SOMEWHERE IN OREGON

Patrick C. Wilkins

Dec. 2010

Patrick C. Wilkins

St. Barthelemy Press, Ltd.

Wilkins, Patrick C.
    Somewhere In Oregon

Cover Artwork: Watercolor by Frank Tuning.
                              Indians fishing at Celilo Falls,
                              ancient fishing grounds on the
                              Columbia River, inundated by back
                              waters of The Dalles Dam.

Chapter Illustrations: Pencil drawings by Frank Tuning.
                              Indian Mystery Rings, Fields' New
                              Street, Lone Pine Dying, Hitler's
                              Trial, Pioneer Grave, Sasquatch,
                              PeeWee Rodeo Champ, Hall Family
                              Cave, Mustangs Range.

Back Cover Portrait: Stro's Photography

Cover Design: Anna McBrayer

Design and Typography: Anna McBrayer

ISBN # 1-887617-07-8

Library of Congress Catalog Card Number: 2001091335

Contents

Contents- continued

Foreword

Some years ago columnist Ann Sullivan wrote in The Oregonian Pat Wilkins was called "the Charles Kuralt of the Northwest." When Kuralt died in 1997, Wilkins himself noted that any "on-the-road" reporter compared to Kuralt had to be "flattered by the association."

But, of course, Pat has always been his own self, and his career goes far beyond the celebrity connected with being a top-notch feature reporter.

My husband, the late Oregon Governor Tom McCall, was an unabashed fan of Pat's "road reports" and told him so. But at the same time, gauged on association that stemmed from the early 1950s, Tom knew that Pat is a reporter's reporter. "In the sense that I am a newsman," declared Tom, "Pat is a newsman." A high compliment from my husband, meaning that Pat is always capable of covering any story, in any situation.

In acknowledging Pat's success reporting on the road, particularly during the last 10 or 15 years of his broadcasting career, it is well to also recognize his earlier accomplishments as news director, anchor, assignment editor, and commentator.

However, I believe Pat's forte has always been his ability to tell "good news" stories with warmth and charm and humor that is absorbing. His motto, in fact, outrageously and intentionally ungrammatical, is telling: "Don't bring me no bad news."

Even in feature reporting, though, it is not possible to avoid all bad news. And it is there that I'm especially impressed with Pat's sensitivity, whether it concerns the death of a tree, as in the chapter "Lone Pine Dying," or the death of my husband, the chapter titled "McCall Was a Friend."

When Pat Wilkins retired from Portland television station KATU in 1990, a coworker exclaimed, "The man's a poet." That truth is also reflected again and again in the pages of this book.

Audrey McCall

Preface

This book perhaps deserves a subtitle because some of its stories range beyond the current borders of the state of Oregon. Even so, the tales are still well within the confines of the old Oregon Territory, so it's not all that much of a stretch.

The Oregon Territory, you'll remember, spread out from the Pacific Ocean to the Rocky Mountains, and from the California border clear to Canada. Then, as now, the area was known as the great Pacific Northwest. That was my beat.

The format: introduction (intro)/story/postscript is meant to reflect the anchor lead/reporter story/anchor tag of TV newscasts—a bow to my career.

The purpose of _Somewhere In Oregon_ (subtitle: On the Road in the Oregon Territory) is the same as was that of the TV reports: to share a tale apart from the hard-life stories, one that makes a person feel lightened up. There's something good about that.

Patrick C. Wilkins

1   Indian Mystery Rings

Intro:

It wasn't just the cold in the predawn sagebrush desert air that made us so alert. We were excited. We were on to something. The summer solstice sunrise could answer the question of whether this giant circle of rocks, stretched out on a barren plateau of sandstone and rimrock, was an ancient astronomical observatory.

We waited, my friends Frank and Myrna Tuning and I, agitated by anticipation that this alignment of rocks, obviously placed by man, must be in the same category as the famous so-called "medicine wheels" found along the eastern fringe of the Rocky Mountains.

This spot, though, was far to the west, in a remote area of Oregon's high desert, practically unknown, and never studied. Its mystery intact, unexplored and unsolved. Then, as the eastern horizon brightened, we became apprehensive. Doubt nagged. It seemed that now, at the last minute, the time of the sunrise might not bear out our optimism of solstice alignment. But we had to be sure; cameras cocked.

The secrets of the site first enticed me in 1984 when Drewsey, Oregon, rancher Glenn Sitz, on whose rangeland the circle is located, showed me the place. The layout of the stones reminded me of an article I had read years before in *National Geographic*.

The working title for the story I did at the time was "Indian Medicine Wheels." The title of record is "Indian Mystery Rings."

The Story:

The mystery is here on a high point, swept by wind and rain; surrounded by sagebrush desert; accented by old, gnarled juniper trees...where we find this giant circle of stones, and other rows of rocks, like spokes leading from hub to rim. All measuring...a guess to be sure...about 40 or 50 feet in diameter.

It's like something we've read about.

Some scientists believe wheels such as this were for the purpose of keeping track of direction and time. For example, standing here in the center, my shadow, in an hour from now, will fall on this line pointing to the north.

It might be one of those mysterious medicine wheels, such as those studied and written about by noted astronomer John Eddy of Boulder, Colorado. Eddy has unlocked the secrets of some. His belief is that they are ancient astronomical observatories.

Dr. Eddy tells us that, if authentic, the Oregon wheel is the farthest west, the only one known west of the Rockies, and in what archaeologists and anthropologists would call a "different culture area."

Rancher Sitz, who led us to this remote spot, says he first stumbled onto the wheel 50 years or more ago. "Evidently, from the chips all around," says Sitz, "this was a place where a lot of people gathered. People who got sorta creative. At least that's how it seems to me."

There are other rings here. Much smaller, but seemingly significant to the larger. And Sitz describes one even larger, some miles from here, where sagebrush has grown up through it.

There are a number of caves here, too. And one imagines the fires that so long ago sooted the walls with black that remains today.

Obsidian and rock chips indicate this was, indeed, a campsite of considerable size. But here and there is evidence that "pot hunters" have already been here, although this is an area where no vehicles travel.

The wheel has survived, it seems, because its only value now is that it remains where it is.

An observatory, perhaps, and crude, to us. A relic, but evidence that long before us there were human beings who had already figured things out.

One can almost feel the presence of those early Indians; one can almost see that presence. Almost....

Postscript:

Finally, I chose the summer solstice of 1997 to determine if the Oregon mystery ring of rocks would match the plains Indians' medicine rings studied by John Eddy.

In the interim between my initial 1984 story and the present, I had learned much more about the Oregon site. I also learned that Dr. Louie Attebery, a professor of English at the Albertson College of Idaho in Caldwell, Idaho, had visited the site years before I did. Attebery says it appears there has been "no serious research" on the site. He calls it a "delightful mystery."

It is located in the Stinking Water Pass area (high plateau), about 40 miles east of Burns, Oregon—an area of lava upcasts, but with flat spaces that appear to be sandstone washed by water erosion. It is on the open spaces on which little or no vegetation grows that the rock circle was laid out. Or, rather, several rock circles . In 1990, on a second trip with Glenn Sitz to the area, he pointed out other rings. He knew about them, of course, but for me it was discovery. (Sitz died in a fire at his home, January 4, 1991).

One large ring of rocks, farthest north, is located on one of the almost-flat areas on top of the upthrust sandstone. I estimated it to be maybe 60 feet in diameter. On another flat close by is a small ring, about nine feet in diameter.

About 200 yards to the south there is another circle (the one that was the subject of my 1984 report, and also our solstice hope) also estimated to be 60 feet in diameter. And lower down, on a gently sloping area, is a smaller ring, perhaps 20 to 30 feet in diameter.

The first two circles are just that...rings of rocks. But the other two are much different. They both have lines of stones, connecting a smaller center ring to the larger circle. Something like spokes in a wheel.

And in the case of the large ring, the spokes join the rim at points where there are even smaller circles of rocks, as if to give these connecting points special emphasis.

This is cattle range, and it seems the animals have occasionally walked through the spoked rings, scattering some of the symmetry. Also, it is evident that harsh winter weather...ice and snow and runoff...has contributed most to deterioration of the layout. In any event, it's difficult to make an accurate count of the number of spokes. But it seems that at the time of their construction, the larger circle must have had at least 20 spokes; perhaps a dozen were built into the smaller.

It does seem that very little of the damage to the rings has been caused by men, although as I've mentioned, there was evidence in 1984 that someone had been digging and sifting in the area. But not directly in the circles.

I reasoned that at least the larger circle seemed to have been laid out to conform to the principal points of direction... north/south, east/west. The smaller spoked ring, in a "flat" sheltered by a curving wall of rock, ranging from about four to ten feet high, might have been similarly oriented. But again, because of the scatter, it would at best be only a guess. And the smaller ring features some rocks much larger than those used in the other construction. A couple of them even suggest an entrance to the ring. They also face directly into the shelter of the wall.

However, it is unlikely that any of the design had anything to do with tipis (tepees). First of all, the pattern is much too large and detailed. And second, what is known of the Paiute Indians who inhabited the area is that their dwellings were not tipis. Instead they built hogans, digging into the earth and utilizing rocks and available vegetation (brush and tree boughs) for building materials.

Two days before the 1997 summer solstice, Frank Tuning accompanied me to the site. Frank had seen the circles only from the air. This was his opportunity to see them up close. And as an artist, to do his own research. Also, in the event my truck couldn't stand up to the torture of the terrible terrain, we'd have company other than coyotes on the long walk back.

The plan was to rediscover the site, take lots of pictures and video, and determine which spokes might match sunrise and sunset of the solstice. We explored an area adjacent to the wheels where Frank discovered a cave I had missed in my previous trips. But most of the day we examined the spoked wheels, concentrating on the big one.

My compass verified that the pattern of the wheel was, sure enough, directional. Along the north/south line of spokes we measured 78 feet, rim to rim. East to west, the tape measure showed 73 feet. A small circle of central "hub" stones was a bit off center either way. But we reasoned the persons who had fashioned this edifice probably did not have a tape measure. And, of course, I also realized my earlier enthusiastic demonstration that the wheel could be used as a sundial was unscientific, and wrong.

Astronomer John Eddy's study of the Rockies' medicine wheels postulated that they were primitive instruments aligned to the solstices. And in particular to the summer solstice, a time for a ritual of the plains Indians known as the sun dance. Eddy's work also detailed, for example, cairns at Wyoming's Bighorn Medicine Wheel that aligned to both the sunrise and sunset. And the rising points of three bright stars: Aldebaran, Rigel, and Sirius.

I hoped for, even expected, comparable performance from the Stinking Water wheel of Harney County, Oregon. It seemed that similar.

We were certain we were on the right track. Discerning the point where time of sunrise would spring onto our wheel, we were delighted to find a spoke of rocks from cairn to cairn, from rim to rim, almost straight across the central hub. We returned to Burns, confident that two days hence, when we again would be positioned here, we would get the proof on the summer solstice's first rays. The meaning of the rest of the wheel's design could be figured out later. We wanted the solstice connection.

On the way to town, a boulder or two along the dim track of lava crust, or perhaps grasping sagebrush, snapped off my truck's road lights. Frank generously offered his wife's big van for the day we would return for the solstice sunrise. It was a vehicle with a lot of clearance, just right for getting over rocks and brush and washouts. It also meant Myrna Tuning would come with us. That, as it turned out, was a stroke of luck.

So, on June 21, 1997, the three of us watched a full moon slowly pale, as the crisp air, maybe 31 degrees, made it plain that it had been a smart move on our part to pull on warm jackets.

I had both my still camera and camcorder at the ready. Both hand held, fearful of losing precious time using tripods. They would hinder fast movement, if rapid place changes became necessary.

A juniper tree was in line with the string of rocks we thought would correspond to the sunrise. The tree surely had grown there after the wheel was placed. And now it would be in the way of the first beams of light of the first

19

day of summer. But we were not concerned. We knew that some of the rays were sure to filter through and the tree's shadow was certain to file along the column. We had as much confidence as if we were scientists.

But..

No sun rays filtered through the tree. The moment was now. No splash of light. Not only not through the juniper, but nowhere on it. Nowhere anywhere on our wheel, either. The sun was not yet up, not risen! What!?...

What?...but yes, that's it. We had not taken into account a ridge immediately in front of us...east...its prominence delaying the sunrise for who knows how long? It would be only minutes, of course, but now the first rays would be all out of whack. What a disappointment!

For a minute or two or three, the sun drifted south, behind the ridge, still refusing, but somehow promising, to deliver. The hills behind us were already bathed in sun-shine, but the horizon we watched was in shadow, almost silhouette. Then there was a flicker, a glimmer and then, almost at once, sunlight. The first flare of summer dashed onto the wheel. But, of course, not through the juniper, nor along our line of hope.

But then..."Look!" an excited exclamation from Myrna. "Look, what's happening." Oh, a wonderful surprise. That first light spilled over the horizon and dashed straight to a V-shaped crevice in the short rimrock. Standing behind the rock wall Myrna could see what appeared to be a miniature eclipse, caused by a round stone lodged in the V, placed so long ago by architects of this site. And looking through the

notch, as if it were an oversized gun sight, squinting directly into the sun, we could see a line of rocks, straight
between the crevice and sun. A line of rocks we earlier had
discounted because they were seemingly scattered, but now
could be seen to be attached to a second, smaller, off-center
hub of the wheel and whose shadows now pointed directly
at the notch with the round stone.

What we were seeing was an alignment that has
occurred for, who knows, how many years...a hundred,
three hundred...more? We could now see what they saw, the
people who built this place.

We had our solstice alignment. We had our Medicine
Wheel! But what did the solstice mean to the prehistoric
people here? Did they, too, have a sun dance? If so, could
that explain the large circle to the north? The one without
any spokes? Was it the place of the dance? The dance
floor!?...delineated by a ring of stones, a circle that was a
symbol of the sun?

The answers have been lost, forever. Lost in time. The
same time still being tracked by this primitive arrangement
of stones, on a high plateau in Oregon.

2   Fields' New Street

Intro:

We were on the way to the Alvord Desert, but we had reservations to stay overnight in Fields, the only place to rent a room in the deep south end of Oregon's Harney County. Photog Bob Foster and I arrived just in time to witness progress come to the remote wayside. And we were invited to join in the celebration, hosted in the welcome shade of a few trees that shielded the party from the summer heat.

Fields, an isolated crossroads for more than a century, finally got a paved street...its only street. A windfall story.

The working title was "Lonely Macadam." The title of record is "Fields' New Street."

The Story:

To appreciate what a paved street means to Fields, Oregon, you have to go back a ways. And that's easy, because the ruins of the stagecoach stop established by Charles Fields back in 1881 are still here, all within sight of the present Fields.

Fields was once an important stop on what was the main route from Winnemucca, Nevada, through what is now the south end of Harney County.

But for most of the last century, residents claim, Fields has been languishing, almost forgotten. But now Fields' only street is being paved. And the three people who live here think it's great.

"What do you think we're having this party for?" laughs Ken Thompson. "Because we're mad?"

Ken and his wife, Julie, are throwing a party for the road crew that is laying down the long-awaited blacktop. The Thompsons own most of the town: the store, the cafe, and what passes as a motel, to which the single street leads.

The cafe boasts two booths, an eight-seat counter, and a display board that, much like McDonald's, flaunts its sales: 2,285 hamburgers in just the last eight months. The store also includes what is claimed to be the smallest liquor department in the state. No public display of sales for booze though.

And a cluttered bulletin board, on which, it is said, there is a picture of founder Charlie Fields with his wife and daughter. It's there, sure enough, a hidden, permanent fixture, but usually found right behind several layers of more recent postings.

Julie Thompson says some people thought "they would never live to see the day that Fields' street would be paved." She admits that there are some other people who never wanted to live to see the day blacktop came to Fields. But for her it's a welcome development, "an end to dust and mud."

24

"Some people in the surrounding area are upset, sad," Julie says. "Although they don't live in Fields, they think a paved street takes away its character."

Ralph Kerr, the town's other resident, says its all for the better. "There's diehards, of course," Kerr snorts, "but if you can't take change you're already dead, aren't ya?"

But progress is coming to more than just Fields in this area. Over the next five years, 60 miles of road will be blacktopped along this route, closing the last gravel gap from here to the Oregon-Nevada border at Denio.

So, what's next for Fields? Parking meters? Street dances? Potholes?

Postscript:

Fields is actually located only 20 miles from Oregon's southern border with Nevada at Denio. But the last section of unimproved road also extended north from Fields to the Roaring Springs Ranch, a distance of 40 miles.

Asphalt spread along the 60 miles means there is now blacktopped highway all the way from Burns, Oregon, to Denio, a distance of 130 miles. The section between Roaring Springs Ranch and Denio is still called by its historic name, the Fields-Denio Road. And despite its newness, it is not anything like a freeway.

The new blacktop bypasses Fields, but so did the old gravel road. Fields' street is a spur that connects with the highway on both ends of the town. In fact, the new road does not entirely bypass Fields, for it courses between the present town and the ruins of the old stagecoach stop.

One night during our stay at Fields it rained for the first time in months. We got rained on. Not because we were caught outside, but because the roof of the "motel" leaked. Apparently, it doesn't rain enough in this area of vast sagebrush desert to detect where a leak is coming from, or often enough to warrant fixing a roof, anyway.

Then there was the matter of a bill. It was either 10 or 12 dollars for snacks I purchased at the store early one morning, as cameraman Bob Foster and I hurried to get to a story at the Alvord Ranch. I remembered I left the money on the counter as we left.

However, the Thompsons remembered me as a deadbeat and sent my company a bill. I urged the company to pay since I conceded my memory of the transaction might be faulty. That was the end of it, I thought.

But years later, while on vacation, I stopped in Fields to get gas. The Thompsons greeted me like old friends, but hit me with the supposed debt again. Not knowing for certain whether the company had actually sent them the money, I paid up again. And yes, I later learned, the company had sent them a check.

By now Ken and Julie have probably caught up on their books. I'll probably be getting a refund. Maybe when I next stop in Fields, at which time I also plan to ask if they've ever fixed that roof.

3 Baker, City of Gold

Intro:

Gold mining literally built the town of Baker City, Oregon. It sprang up in 1864 around a mill set on the Powder River especially to process quartz ore from the rich Virtue Mine, which was more than ten miles away and had inadequate water on-site to do the job.

Baker City had the accidental good fortune to be located almost in the center of the eastern Oregon gold fields of the late 1800s. And it soon became both the financial center and county seat. Both the town and the county were named for Colonel Edward Baker, who was Oregon's first U.S. Senator and a hero of the Mexican and Civil Wars (Baker was killed at the battle of Ball's Bluff, Virginia), and once a law partner, political opponent, and friend of Abraham Lincoln. (Lincoln named his youngest son, Eddie, after Baker.)

In 1911 the town dropped City from its name and became justplain Baker but changed back again in 1989 to reclaim its historic image and draw attention to the town's gold-fever past. During the 78-year interim the town's economy changed to one of farming, ranching, and timber.

Gold, however, is its heritage. And there are prospectors pecking at the old digs all the time. As luck would have it, one of those prospectors made a big, new gold discovery there in 1984, right in town. An exclusive!

The working title for the story was "Eureka!" The title of record is "Baker, City of Gold."

The Story:

Eureka! Baker is a city of gold. Both figuratively and literally. The gold rush of the late 1800s built the town. But now it's been discovered that a good part of the town was built of gold.

All its major buildings, constructed around the turn of the century, were unknowingly built of gold-bearing volcanic tuff.

The person who made the discovery, geologist Neil Isaacson of La Grande, Oregon, estimates there may be a quarter-of-a-million dollars worth of gold and silver in the stone walls of downtown Baker buildings.

After pacing off dimensions of the 80-year-old City Hall, Isaacson told Mayor Bill Gwilliam it alone contains over $30,000 worth of gold.

The Mayor was surprised, but joked, "Well, nobody wants to get rid of it, maybe that's why."

Isaacson says his estimates are based on today's price for gold. And what he has learned about the pits where the building stone was quarried. The material came from several quarries located at Pleasant Valley, ten miles south of Baker. Isaacson says at turn-of-the-century gold values it would not have been profitable to mine then, even if the gold were known to be there. Today the ore is worth something over 80 dollars a ton

It was "black patina" on some Baker buildings that tipped Isaacson off, and sent him searching for the source of the stone. "It looked like magnesium or silver mineralization," he says, "and they're generally in company with gold."

His assessment of the quarries?

"There's probably at least 10 million tons of this ore there," he says. "And possibly as high as 40 million tons of ore that would be of commercial grade."

Among other Baker structures made of the ore are: the county courthouse, which Isaacson estimates contains about $35,000 worth of gold; the St. Francis Catholic Church, about $65,000; the old hospital, now a nursing home, about $56,000; the Pythian Building, which now houses a CPA firm, about $25,000.

But a private home, worth about $4,800 as gold ore, points up that these buildings are not about to be "mined" for their gold content. First of all, they are history. But more important, they are more valuable as real estate.

Theresa Johnson, who is trying to sell, jokes, "I'll make sure and add that to the price of the house."

The reaction to all this is mild shock, from which the town is sure to rapidly recover. But from now on, it's also sure to be a talking point in the history of Baker.

Postscript:

The biggest boost in gold activity, in claim registry and mining since the early days, actually came in 1979 when the price of goldskyrocketed. The price shot up to $400 an ounce, then over $500. In the following year, the price climbed to $850 before it backed off and hovered around an average $600 an ounce.

It was a heady period in Baker. At least half a dozen major companies were doing development work or actually operating mines. The local employment office disclosed that at least 200 crewmen were working the claims.

Cameraman Chuck Von Wald and I thought it would take no more than a couple of days to produce a good feature about the new gold rush. But we were overwhelmed. Gold stories were everywhere. We got excited. Those two days stretched to two weeks, two weeks in which we sent back a report a day to Channel 2.

We ranged from the Elkhorn Ridge of the Blue Mountains to the west to Hells Canyon and the Wallowa Mountains to the east. There was Mormon Basin, then Granite, Sumpter, Halfway, Cornucopia, Flagstaff, Iron Dike, and others...all old gold strikes that were being worked again. The daily reports aired on our newscasts were produced into a half-hour documentary we called "The '79ers."

The renewed gold activity, however, was transient...only a blip on the Baker County economy. The economy is still based largely on farming, ranching, and timber. And now, Oregon Trail tourism.

4   Lone Pine Dying

Intro:

Much of Oregon was being seared by drought in 1977. Tough to believe in a state where rain is so constant it is said people rust instead of tan. But that's in winter, mostly. Well...actually, there is a lot of rain in spring and fall, too. But in summer, things dry out a little.

In that summer, things dried up. The reservoirs were thirsty, deprived of runoff so that normal shorelines stood far above water levels. Some reservoirs were so low that debris buried beneath the water, cast out from boats, the stuff people thought they would never see again, safely out of sight and mind, was exposed. Cans, bottles, clothing, snagged fishing lures lying there accusingly, on muddy bottoms, newly revealed by the desiccation.

In some areas cutting back on water use was voluntary, in others decreed. But it was not long before people started rusting again. The rains came.

There were few life-or-death casualties of the dry spell. But one of them was a famous landmark at The Dalles: a natural-growth pine tree, rooted in an improbable place.

The working title for the story was "Parched Pine." The title of record is "Lone Pine Dying."

The Story:

The Lone Pine is dying...wasting away on a massive rocky ledge of the Columbia River, only a few yards from the ghostly remains of the aged Indian settlement houses and Shaker church built in 1891.

The Lone Pine gasps for life for want of water, just a few feet from the river and fewer than 30 yards from the ornate swimming pool of a modern motel.

The tree is hardly 25 feet high, almost a scrub as pines go. But a veritable giant in a climate that allows little more than sagebrush to grow.

More than that, this tree has given its name to one of the so-called "in lieu" Indian fishing sites on the Columbia River, granted to treaty Indians when dams inundated their traditional fishing grounds. The platforms from which the Indians swing their dip nets hang from the basalt face of what is called the Lone Pine fishing site.

And a nearby restaurant has chosen the name Lone Pine to display on a sign twice as tall as the tree.

The motel management became concerned about the Lone Pine's health late last summer and called in Wasco County extension agent Jack Thines. His prescription? Give it lots of water. But it apparently came too late.

"Frankly," says Thines, "I think that tree's not going to make it." It was deceptively green long after it actually became desperately in need of moisture, it seems, so no one was aware of that need.

"It's a shame," declared Thines, "the drought was more

than it could stand."

And, as we've already pointed out, the Lone Pine is not just a tree, it is history here. And if it dies, it will be sorely missed.

Postscript:

The Lone Pine's health continued to deteriorate. Its needles slowly turned from green to brown, much like some of the needles did seasonally to make way for new growth. But an evergreen pine never loses all its foliage at once, unless it is terribly sick or dying. Lone Pine was now both.

All its needles changed, converted to its bark tinge, now looking dead, and surely dead. Then storms howled in from the west and banged over the escarpments just downriver, the winds plucking the needles at will. Thrown they were, helter-skelter, as if they were simply leaves. And meant to be tossed about when dead.

The Lone Pine stood its ground. An upright skeleton tree, a reminder of both its life and death, its own tombstone. Stood up to the winds for years. But dry rot became a cancer that spread through its footing and weakened its strength. On a bright summer day touched by a breeze as light as nature can sigh, the Lone Pine crumbled at its base, leaving not even a stump, and fell to the ground.

It lay there, returning to earth, long after another tree was planted to take its place.

5   Chicken Whistle Creek

Intro:

It was Chicken Little who ran around screaming that the sky was falling. So we all know that chickens can talk. But for some reason we don't believe chickens can whistle. At least some of us don't. Among the non-believers is Bel Ivey of Veneta, Oregon. Still, some years ago, she championed "chicken whistle" as the name for a creek. Why?

Well, Oregon is full of Deer Creeks, Rock Creeks and Bear Creeks...even a Rattlesnake Creek or two. But is there a Chicken Whistle Creek? No, there is none. But according to Bel Ivey there should be. Cameraman Mark Plut and I wandered a backwoods road trying to find the Ivey place. Lost...but then we heard a whistle.

No, not a chicken whistle. A Bel whistle, telling us we had arrived.

The working title for the story was "The Sky is Falling." The title of record is "Chicken Whistle Creek."

The Story:

High on a razorback ridge near Veneta, Oregon, Bel and Chuck Ivey have leveled a space they call a farm. More accurately, Chicken Whistle Farm. And far down a precipitous slope that slants over most of their 3 1/2 acres, they've found a trickle of water. Getting to it, Bel says, "Takes some figuring, how to make the descent without expending your total energy output for the day."

And what's down here is an unnamed creek. "Okay this is it." Where? "Right here." A dribble of water, a leak in the rocks. But not really lazy like an ooze, instead gushing like a...maybe, like a creek.

Sometimes you must not laugh, but remember. Remember that great rivers like the Columbia, the Niagara, the Mississippi, all have small beginnings.

So this rivulet, according to Bel, must have a name. And it must be Chicken Whistle. "I've spent a lot of time with chickens," says Bel, "and I've really enjoyed them. And they've been good friends and pets through the years." She admits, though, she has never heard a chicken whistle. And that symbolically indicates the small size of the farm. "And passing the name on to the creek is just the right thing to do."

Don't think that Bel and Chuck aren't serious. Why, after tumbling along the ravine for less than a mile, this water joins up with Battle Creek and really begins to hum.

And Battle Creek carries on a little farther and pours into Coyote Creek, and now it's a chorus of babbling brooks.

And Coyote Creek dumps it all into Fern Ridge Reservoir, helping that body of water build up its strength.

In that mix, Chicken Little Whistle...no...little Chicken Whistle Creek is a year-round contributor. And, by golly, Bel feels the name should stick, be made official. The

38

request has gotten as far as the Oregon Geographic Names Board, part of the Oregon Historical Society.

"I always thought they were in charge of antiquities and history, and that sort of thing," she says. "I didn't realize that they were also in the business of handing out names."

Bel's idea might be whimsy to some, but seems to be contagious. Initial reaction from board members indicated they enjoyed the proposal. But official action won't be taken for awhile. Board members are busy right now, helping to celebrate the bicentennial observance of Captain Robert Gray's Pacific Coast explorations.

Gray's principal discovery, of course, was the mighty river of the west, which, by the way, he did not need a board to help him name. He simply named it after his ship...the Columbia. (Columbia Rediviva.)

The Board will meet next in August. And that's when we'll probably next hear about the naming of Chicken Whistle Creek.

Postscript:

Naming things geographic apparently takes some time. It was over two years later that the Iveys learned the outcome of their request. In a letter dated May 3, 1990, the Oregon Geographic Names Board informed the Iveys that the members had approved the proposal. And that the decision had been passed on to the U.S. Board on Geographic Names in Reston, Virginia.

And that was that, except there is a time lag of eight

years between approval and placement on maps. But the Iveys are happy. The name Chicken Whistle Creek made it. Whether or not anyone ever hears a whistling chicken.

6   Teapot Station

There's an intriguing speck on the horizon. It looks like a teapot! A teapot? The closer we get, the surer we get. Something like deciphering the scene in Lawrence of Arabia where a speck on the horizon slowly becomes a camel and rider. Closer yet, the teapot is a giant as teapots go, but is also a small building.

Soon, signs tell us what we think we already know. We're at Zillah, Washington, and we've come upon the Teapot Dome service station. Photog Bob Foster smiles smugly, "Another story has just dropped into our lap."

The working title for the story was "Two for Teapot." The title of record is "Teapot Station."

The Story:

Motorists who leave Interstate 82 at Zillah, Washington, looking for gasoline, also wind up getting a history lesson at the Teapot Dome station.

If you're hazy about details of the Teapot Dome oil scandal of the Warren Harding administration, station owner Dick Thomas can fill you in, while filling you up. Thomas tells customers, who want to know, that is...like Canadian Merv Wright...the scandal involved Wyoming oil leases and Harding's Secretary of the Interior, Albert Fall.

"Basically, what he did was lease that property to people for the oil rights," teaches Thomas, "then he just backed up and took kickbacks."

The lesson also includes information that Thomas's mother is among the people who still remember the uproar. "She says it was every bit as big as Watergate." And Dick knows the mess was called the Teapot Dome because of a rock on the site of the leases that resembled a teapot.

The station was built back in 1922 in dubious honor of that scandal. Dick's father bought the station in 1928. But in 1977, after Dick took over, trouble brewed.

The Washington Department of Transportation was pushing the freeway through, and the station had to be relocated. Thomas says the department agreed to relocate the Dome in a "short period of time." He expected it to be about 90 days.

"Their interpretation apparently was any time they darn well wanted to do it," laments Thomas. The controversy over the delay was heated. "They finally did it, but it was over seven years later."

Two years ago the station got back in business and the business has taken hold. The building is also on the National Register of Historic Places. And road signs alert motorists to that fact. The station is also a small convenience store.

But the sturdy old outhouse can't be used. It would take about $16,000 to bring it up to modern code. That irks Dick because a much smaller modern outhouse, a port-a-potty, does fit the code.

But the Teapot's business is bubbling, what with its own T-shirts, postcards, bumper stickers, and coffee cups that can double as tea cups.

Dick brags he has the "world's most unique service station." And in this part of the world, at least, he's probably right.

Postscript:

Dick Thomas, a school teacher and administrator for 30 years, now leases the Teapot to another operator because "no other family member seems interested in taking it over."

But the port-a-potty is still part of the service, and the old outhouse is still part of the picture. The shape of the station building, of course, remains a teapot.

7   IRS Says So

Intro:

Did you ever find a dime or quarter or dollar bill and simply slip it into your pocket and forget about it? Well, according to the Internal Revenue Service, you're not supposed to do that. "Found money," says the IRS, "is regarded as income." And you should declare it on your income tax return. Otherwise, you're a tax cheat.

The working title for the story was "IRS Says So." The title of record is also "IRS Says So."

The Story:

For the past year I've very carefully kept track of money I've found and money that was given to me. For openers, I've learned that people are far more careless with money than they are generous with money.

You see, the "found" money totals up to $2.69; the "given" money just a dollar and 30 cents. Of course my vigilance is a major factor in finding so much money. The rule is: Keep your eyes on the ground. But simply keeping my eyes on the ground is only part of it.

True, I find money everywhere. Tops...a 25-cent piece in the parking lot of the Marine Science Center in Newport, Oregon. Pennies, in a lot of places: one cent on a picnic table at Promontory Park near Estacada, 18 pennies in my recovered stolen car...two under a mat on the passenger side, one in the glove compartment, the rest in the fender well on the right side, inside the trunk.

And people sometimes forget and leave change in the coin return slots of telephones and food machines. Well, I can't go around trying to run down the owner, so I've simply added it to the found-money pile. I took the vanes out of the clothes dryer to clean the lint away from the drum, and I found some nickels and dimes.

But now I have a problem. A problem that a lot of people advise, "forget it." But not me. I've got a conscience as big as the Federal Building in Portland. So, I went to talk to the Internal Revenue Service about possible taxes on this found and given money.

"We don't need to know where you found the money," says IRS agent Mary Lee Planer, "just that you be sure and declare it." It's just added onto total income. So, you pay taxes on that.

"The good news," she says, "is that any money you have received as a gift is not regarded as income and is not taxable." What if someone, say, gives me a million dollars? "You would not have to pay taxes on it." She was firm about that.

If you found a million dollars, that's much different. That's income. Uncle Sam would take a big bite. The long and short of it is that if you don't declare "found" money, you're cheating on your income tax.

And that ain't the American way!...is it?

Postscript:

Don't think for an instant the Internal Revenue Service has overlooked "given" money. A gift of a million dollars would not go unnoticed or untaxed.

The accountant who does my income tax returns does assure me that if some benefactor wrote me a check for a million, it would be all mine...no tax. But the IRS, he says, works backward to nip the giver. For the beneficent action of making me a millionaire, my patron would have to come up with hundreds of thousands in taxes. See?

There is no escape.

8   Corvair Lair

Intro:

In the early 1960s my brother, Graham Wilkins, bought a brand new rear-engine car put out by General Motors. It was called the Corvair. Graham had owned a number of Volkswagens he drove on his rural mail route. So, when he purchased the Corvair, he was not a rear-engine virgin. He knew how to drive such a car.

But this new automobile, looking more like a box than a beetle, challenged him. He was surprised by the sensation you got that the front wheels were almost off the ground, as if you were driving an overloaded pickup truck. In less than a month, the car spun out twice, both times when it was packed with his family.

"A deathtrap," was how my brother described it, ahead of Ralph Nader. He couldn't wait of get rid of it.

Still, despite my brother's opinion and that of Ralph Nader, who derided the Corvair in a book he called _Unsafe at Any Speed_, the Corvair was produced for nearly a decade. And all along, there was ample evidence not everyone agreed with the critics. People bought them.

Among the buyers was Norman Welch of Connell, Washington. Even years after the Corvair was dropped from the General Motors stable, Welch continued to buy. He, and many others, now considered the Corvair a car collector's prize. A classic.

The working title for the story was "Corvairs Galore." The title of record is "Corvair Lair."

The Story:

Ralph Nader might get the chills from a collection of cars on a Connell, Washington farm. They're all Corvairs.

Norman Welch has over 130 Chevrolet Corvairs on his 2,400-acre farm at Connell. The controversial vehicle General Motors manufactured from 1960 to 1969 was the first American-built car with a rear-mounted engine. It was G.M.'s answer to the Volkswagen.

But along came consumer advocate Ralph Nader, who in 1963 picked the Corvair to pieces, citing it as one of the worst attempts to build a quality automobile in American history. Unsafe at any speed, he wrote, and talked a lot about how people got killed because of the car's peculiar handling characteristics.

But Norman Welch says he bought his first Corvair because he was impressed with the way it handled. "The early ones might have been a little touchy," Welch says. "Because they were new to the public, they were a new concept, the engine was in the rear and it changed the way a car handled."

It was this unfamiliarity with how the new car had to be driven, Welch believes, that accounted for early accidents. "When the public got used to Corvairs," he says, "things improved." Then in 1965 the car was redesigned and, according to Welch, "I don't think there was a better-handling car on the market."

Welch says that while the Corvair was killed off by Nader, the Corvair was good to Nader. "It launched his career."

Since buying his first Corvair, Welch has gone about the region snapping up others. He's even saved them from being crushed into scrap by wrecking yards. "I got 10 and 12 at a time that way," he says. He figures he has every model of Corvair built, including vans and pickups. A few are "drivers"; most are restorable.

Norm bought one for five dollars, another for $600. Most were purchased at a time when they were inexpensive to collect. Some he got for hundreds, are now valued at thousands of dollars.

His intent all along has been to fix them all up. "But I suddenly realized," he says, "that I don't have enough time to fix up all the cars I have around here, so I don't know what I'm going to do with them."

Norm keeps about 50 of what he calls his "special" Corvairs in a barn; ones which could be running in no time. He says although he has traded and sold some, and plans to continue, he will not sell any parts. The way he puts it, "I won't tear them apart the way that guy Nader did. I bought them to save them."

Postscript:

Today there are Corvair owners' clubs across the country. And while not many members own as many Corvairs as Welch, many do own more than one. A few years ago Ralph Nader even accepted an invitation to attend and speak at a National Convention of Corvair Owners. He was amiable, but unrepentant.

9   The Measure of Moody

Intro:

The name Zenas Ferry Moody probably doesn't mean much to anybody but Oregonians. And just as probable, not many Oregonians know more than the fact that Moody was Oregon's seventh Governor.

But Moody was involved in a project that, even today, touches the lives of everybody who lives in the Northwest.

That involvement was one of a six-part series cameraman Stan Killingsworth and I produced and reported for Oregon's 125th statehood anniversary. Both the working and record title for the series was "Oregon, My Oregon." One part is "The Measure of Moody."

The Story:

The textbook image of Zenas Moody is largely that of · what he did as Governor from 1882 to 1887. He even served two extra months when the legislature changed its meeting time. But what really sets Zenas Moody apart is that he was a member of the crew that in 1851 to 1853 surveyed the vast Oregon Territory.

Moody himself never made much of his part in the survey. He joined the crew as a "chainman," shortly after it started work following his arrival from Massachusetts. He apparently took the job to make ends meet while he set his own course.

Moody was actually only a laborer on the team. But for the time, wages must have been fairly good. It was during the period of the gold rush, and the leader had a terrible time hiring a crew. It was a time when carpenters were getting eight dollars a day, butter was selling for 75 cents a pound and flour was 15 dollars a barrel. The cost of provisions for the survey party, obviously, was high. And common laborers wanted $75 to $100 a month in wages.

Somehow, the party managed to work within the money budgeted by Congress the year before. And two crews...one east-west, the other north-south...traveled the terrain for the next couple of years.

Because of Indian hostility, the northern crew was protected by armed guards. And, where terrain was impassable, the crews did some guessing. But at the end, the lines of the Willamette Meridian were set.

Moody went on to distinguish himself beyond laborer in the band that delineated those lines, culminating in the governorship in 1882. Along the way, he prospered in the mercantile business; he was a storekeeper who founded the town of Umatilla, Oregon, to be closer to, and thereby better able to supply, the gold mines in a region that included Idaho.

Moody fathered five children. Two sons served in Congress.

While governor, among the things Moody wanted from the legislature were legislative reapportionment, tax base, safeguards for the ballot box, separation of juvenile offenders from hardened criminals, an office of attorney general, and a stringent law against carrying concealed weapons. Moody did not get them all, but all are now part of Oregon law.

In his last years Moody recounted much of his life for a newspaper reporter. He skimmed over his part in the Northwest survey. In light of his menial job with the survey crew, and his later accomplishments...that is understandable. But in terms of today, he played a role in taking the most important measurements ever done in the region.

Every building, every road, every bridge, every airport runway, every property line that exists today, and every change made by every survey crew today, is based on the lines set out by the Willamette Meridian party.

This secluded glen in the west hills of Portland is the starting point of that survey. And this is the Willamette Stone that marks the meridian and base lines. From here the lines stretch west to the Pacific, east to the Rocky Mountains, south to California, and north...clear to Canada.

And in this time, every single day, every single person is affected by those boundaries. Each of us. All of us.

Postscript:

Some years later vandals broke off and stole the Willamette Meridian Stone from the little, secluded park set aside to honor the survey. It was senseless, as vandalism always is. It was malicious destruction of a shrine. It hurt.

The durable Willamette Stone had replaced the cedar

post which originally marked the starting point of the survey. Of course another marker was put in place following the theft. But everybody knows that historically the Stone was irreplaceable.

10   Hitler's Trial

Just a few months after Neil Armstrong became the first man to walk on the moon, the people of North Plains, Oregon, got something new to talk about: Hitler.

Soon the buzz in the small farm community, 20 miles west of Portland, got so loud that it was heard across the nation. The story was so important, in fact, that the assignment desk advised me to get on the story and stay on it, or run the risk of being "aced out by Kuralt."

I can't remember if Charles Kuralt actually ever did the story as one of his On the Road reports, but I do know that it was one on which we did not eat his dust.

I did the story for Channel Two, of course, and also for ABC. The working title for the report was "Sic 'Em." The title of record is "Hitler's Trial."

The Story:

Hitler didn't look like a mutt exactly, maybe a little bit of a lot of other ancestry, but mostly he looked German shepherd. There never was any doubt he was named for his mostly look. There was no comparison, though, to that other Hitler, his namesake.

Hitler, the mostly German shepherd dog, didn't have a

mean bone in his body.

But he did break the law.

Hitler lived in a tiny Oregon town called North Plains, the kind of town that's so small you can drive through it before you can slow down to the speed limit. For 10 years Hitler had free run of the place, and everybody knew him by name. And although he could go anywhere he wanted to, he mainly wandered back and forth between the town's two main street taverns. The saloons had names, too, of course, but most people simply referred to them as the "Upper" and "Lower" taverns, since one of them was at the top of a slight hill and the other at the bottom. Hitler hung out at one or the other of the taverns most of the time.

The owners and customers alike fed Hitler. And a few of them tried to get him to drink beer, but he didn't seem to like the stuff. No one ever saw him drunk.

Instead, he came for the handouts of food and candy. And in return he allowed himself to be petted. He came to expect the freebies and the people came to expect his visits.

Hitler was truly living a dog's life.

Suddenly, though, Hitler's idle was interrupted. Without any warning, at least to Hitler, and perhaps to some North Plains people, county authorities came down hard...really hard...on Hitler. Hitler, they said, was breaking the law, running loose in violation of a brand-new dog leash ordinance.

Some folks said they had never heard of such a thing, and even if there were such a law, they reasoned, it certainly didn't apply to North Plains. And, in particular, surely not to Hitler.

But the town council, more than a year before, <u>had</u> signed an agreement with the county for dog control. So, there it was, an awful threat to Hitler's way of life. Would he remain free or be restrained...even confined?

He continued to roam.

It is not known who first blew the whistle on Hitler, or if it was just the result of zealous enforcement of the law, that led to his initial arrest. Jailed! And then not just once, but several times. But he was bailed out of every one of the impoundments. It wasn't like he was going to skip the country or something. He was a town dog, a small-town town dog who had never ever been, as far as anyone knew, outside the city limits, except when he was taken into custody.

It was bewildering to Hitler, undoubtedly, especially when he had memories of growing up in a service station and coming and going as he pleased. And being affectionately known as "everybody's dog." The worst anybody ever called him was the "town mutt." And sure, everybody called him Hitler, because that was his name, and of course he had no idea that Hitler was a name not many dogs would want, if they had a choice.

Sam Bass...yes, Sam Bass...was Hitler's main benefactor.

Some could maybe make something out of that name, too, but everyone who knew Bass knew they'd better not. He was a tall, lanky cowboy who seemed like he wouldn't take too well to being kidded. In truth, he did appear to

have some of the rough edges of the infamous frontier ban-
dit of the same name. But it would be wrong to assume that
North Plains's Sam Bass was any relation to the Sam Bass
shot dead by Texas Rangers way back in 1878. And even if
he were kin, Bass didn't seem to be carrying a grudge
against anyone...except the dogcatchers.

There was a toughness there all right that was outright
contradictory to the tenderness he lavished on Hitler, but
which was consistent with action he took to protect Hitler's
freedom. Yet Bass denied he was Hitler's owner, said he
was just a friend.

But the friendship was special.

That's because one night a couple of hooligans jumped
Bass and Hitler leapt into the brawl on Bass's side. "Hitler
saved my life," he said. The stuff of binding friendships.

But in the process of bailing his friend out of the dog
pound, in return rescuing him from possible death, a step
ahead of Hitler's being "put to sleep," Bass got in trouble,
too. He was cited for failing to buy a license for Hitler.

This happened about the same time Bass was heading
up a petition drive to have Hitler declared town property
and free from the leash law. And while there were frequent
strategy sessions at both the Upper and Lower taverns, there
were some people who said they thought "the law is the
law" and Hitler ought to be tied up.

One of them was Police Chief Eugene Shaw, who said
he liked Hitler a lot, but "the law should be applied equally" to all dogs. What a blow that was, especially in light of
the fact that Shaw was also a service station operator. But

obviously not operator of the station where Hitler grew up.

And there was also the consequence that Hitler's confinement had made him really edgy, almost paranoid. He distrusted all strangers, and found it difficult to even warm up to journalists who came to report his story. His friends said, because he could not, that it was because he feared strangers were dogcatchers. Hitler often relaxed and would sometimes shake hands, though, after his companions explained to him there was no cause for concern.

Then too, there was the inability of some reporters to accurately pin down Sam Bass. He was alternately called an "ex-cattleman," a "cattle buyer," a "sometime bartender," when he obviously was a cowboy. He wore a big gray Stetson, a western shirt, Levis, cowboy boots, and a big, silver belt buckle. And even though Hitler once saved his butt in a fight, you could tell Bass probably liked to fight. You know, a cowboy.

So that might be at least part of the reason he took up the battle of freedom for Hitler. A good fight.

Soon Hitler went on trial. That is, Sam Bass went on trial. The issue, of course, was that delayed license and delinquency charge, the running-loose thing. Even the justice, Municipal Judge Vernon Richards, indicated that although it was Bass who was on trial, the trial was really about Hitler himself.

Eighty people crowded into the tiny North Plains courtroom to witness the case unfold when Bass arrived with Hitler...on a leash. It was a brash protest, not capitulation.

Hitler's appearance in the courtroom provoked expressions of familiarity from many of the spectators, but his stay was short-lived. Judge Richards ordered the dog removed. The judge also followed another of the then orthodox court prerogatives. He threw press cameramen out.

With Hitler and the photogs out of the way the hearing began.

The six-member jury included a dog owner, a woman who had a cat she said she didn't like, and a chinchilla farmer. There were only two witnesses, dogcatcher Roy Patrick and Bass.

Patrick testified that Bass had paid six dollars the previous year for a license and a delinquency charge after Hitler was picked up for running loose. City Attorney DeMar Batchelor told the jury that constituted ownership of Hitler by Bass.

Not so, according to Bass, who contended he was acting only as a sort of bail bondsman for the dog. "I bailed him out," said Bass, "took him back to where he'd been picked up and dumped him out." And then, as Bass's testimony continued, some of the onlookers could tell he had a lump in his throat. "I did it because ol' Hitler has did me a couple of good turns," Bass said, "and he shakes my hand once in a while."

Good grief...after that, it took the jury only an hour and a half to find Bass not guilty. The packed courtroom applauded the decision.

Just outside, Hitler, who had snoozed through the trial, was awakened by the commotion. Minutes later, after dispatching an itch with a few rapid strokes of a hind leg, he shook hands with defense attorney Thomas Kerrigan and accepted congratulations of well-wishers.

Not guilty!

But...that wasn't the end of it.

Hitler's forces knew that the dog-control authorities thought the whole issue was silly; that the law had been mocked, circumvented for fun; that the proceedings were a circus. They were not amused. They warned that the dog leash law would continue to be enforced indiscriminately. Look out, Hitler.

So Hitler volunteers organized a sort of early detection warning system, headquartered at the town's Lower tavern, to keep a watchful eye out for the dogcatcher. The system, as it turned out, was myopic.

Hitler was again snatched.

But this time, so stealthily that for days his whereabouts were unknown. There was some thought that Hitler's celebrity had attracted dognappers. There was no ransom note, but, of course, there was also the possibility that whoever took Hitler simply wanted to own a dog who was famous. Sam Bass said Hitler was just getting used to living in a new doghouse, placed at the rear of the Lower tavern. And Bass discovered there an empty dog food can of a strange brand and signs of a struggle. There was a single telephone call demanding 100 dollars for Hitler's return. Bass said he went to the location designated for the payoff, but no one showed up.

North Plains was shaken.

But no...it soon came out that the dog-control officers

65

were up to their old tricks. They had Hitler back in custody, under the same old charge...running loose, at large.

But they made a mistake. He was not incarcerated in the official jail...the dog pound...but at a private kennel. They compounded the mistake by first denying they had taken Hitler, then admitting the truth, but then claiming he was transferred to a veterinarian's kennel because there was overcrowding and no room for him at the pound.

All this secrecy, holding Hitler incognito and incommunicado and moving him from one facility to another, apparently to keep his friends from finding him, reeked of the stuff for which habeas corpus was written.

So a writ of habeas corpus for Hitler was filed in the county's circuit court by Tom Kerrigan, the very same lawyer who represented Sam Bass at Hitler's trial. The difference was that now Kerrigan was directly representing Hitler.

In the petition Kerrigan said Hitler was being held at an unknown location "without virtue of any judgment or decree against him." And that the reason for his "imprisonment is unknown." Typical habeas corpus language. County Judge Hollie Pihl set a date for a hearing on the writ, at which time the county's top dog-control officer would have to make known the cause of the arrest.

Meanwhile, Hitler was allowed to pose for news cameras at his place of confinement...or rather...one of his places of confinement. It was comforting for his supporters to know that he was alive and well. No euthanasia tank, yet. Hitler wagged his tail a lot, apparently confident about what the outcome of the habeas corpus hearing would be.

Hitler's last stand was fought in the court of no-non-sense Circuit Court Judge Albert Musick. Hitler's friends were there. Sam Bass was there. Hitler was not there. Still jailed. The judge, who might have been sure there were more important judicial matters to adjudicate, could have said: "If you think for a minute this court will play along with this frivolity, you're barking up the wrong tree." He didn't. But he did admonish that the Hitler saga "has gone on far enough."

However, county attorney Richard Roberts was vexed. "It is distressing to me, as an attorney," he declared, "to be part of a possibility of turning a court into a zoo or circus." Roberts also asserted it was almost absurd to have to argue the issue. But he did. He argued that Hitler was not a person and therefore not eligible for privileges of habeas corpus. He asked that the writ be quashed. Roberts did it with a straight face, ignoring the fact he was going to have a pleasant conversation starter for all the rest of his life.

Hitler's lawyer, Tom Kerrigan, assured the court that Hitler was no joke, "the action not taken in jest." Particularly since there had been apparent attempt by county dog control to hold his client in secret. Kerrigan argued that under our law, dogs have traditionally been treated differently than other animals; that Hitler, in fact, had been treated by some citizens of North Plains as a citizen of that community.

And that the Oregon statute on habeas corpus leaves

open to question its use in behalf of something other than a person.

But Judge Musick sided with Roberts. "You can't make a member of the canine a person by calling him one."

And along that line of reasoning Hitler was not a person and was not entitled to habeas corpus. However, hizzoner further stated he deplored that some members of the human race run rampant and act as wild beasts, and often have more fault than domestic animals, such as Hitler.

But then the judge looked right at Sam Bass. "If someone with enough guts comes forward to claim the dog," he said, "and will be responsible for him and keep him from running at large, then he will be released." Sam Bass was it.

A short time later, after the cowboy transferred the dog's license to his own name, he and Hitler were reunited. A union that demanded, under law, that they be inseparable, linked by a leash. So Hitler was sprung. And the establishment had demonstrated that law and order, even in the form of a dog leash law, was important enough to enforce.

Hitler lived out his days at his bunker in back of the tavern. Along the way tavern owner Peggy Crebs took over responsibility for him. At times Hitler had to give up his doghouse because an occasional wino would want to sleep in it. So he spent a lot of time lounging where he could. In the tavern. On the sidewalk. Here and there.

And he often got from here to there and back without a leash. The same kind of roaming that got him locked up before but now went unnoticed, at least unchallenged. Times and attitudes change.

But it remains that everywhere in the world where the

name Hitler is spoken the name is synonymous with a member of the human race who ran rampant and acted as a wild beast.

But Hitler is a name that, at least in North Plains, also means "a man's best friend." A gentle dog. A fight for freedom.

Postscript:

Where is Hitler's grave? I wanted to know so I dropped in at the the old Deak and Peg's tavern in North Plains, where Hitler used to hang out.

The pub is now called Morrow's Corner, but it's still the same small brick building it's always been, although the building hasn't always been a tavern. Originally it was a bank, a small bank. And it's kept much the same as it's always been because it's a historical landmark.

North Plains used to be smaller, too, but during ensuing years it has grown. During Hitler's time here there used to be a population of about 600; it's now more than double that. But apparently the thirst of the town hasn't doubled. There's only a few people at the bar at mid-afternoon.

The place hasn't changed all that much since the last time I saw its insides, years ago. Oh, there're some of those gambling, or as the promoters of gambling like to call then, "gaming" machines. But it still has the quaint, frontier-like look I carried in my memory, from the Hitler days.

"Hitler was before my time," said owner Leon Morrow,

"but my mother, who owned this place for 18 years, knows all about him. She can tell you."

From a patron, "Or, how about Dick and Bobbie Boyer?"

What I wanted to know was: when did Hitler die? How did he die? Was he buried or cremated? Where's his grave? Questions that some of the old-timers probably could answer.

Unfortunately, most of those old-timers are dead, too. And some of them, like the Boyers, who are still alive and well and who still regard Hitler's old haunt as their favorite place to sip a beer, are kinda fuzzy about remembering details like that.

"We remember that old Hitler, sure enough," said Dick Boyer. His wife, Bobbie, nodded confirmation. "But we just don't know what happened to him. Wait'll Francis gets here. She knows all about Hitler."

How about others who knew Hitler?

Peggy? Passed on.

Deak? Also dead.

Sam? Gone and buried.

Francis Morrow? "Hitler?" she said, "he was gone before I bought the tavern." But she remembered, "He really stirred up the county back in '70." That's all, though.

"Talk to Bill Duyck," Mrs. Morrow added. "His uncle, Bill O'Connell, owned the service station where Hitler lived."

Uncle Bill? Dead.

"Talk to Eugene Shaw," Duyck urged, "he was the

police chief during that Hitler mess. He'll sure know."

Eugene Shaw was less sure. "I stayed out of that Hitler thing, pretty much."

I reminded him that during the Hitler trouble he, Shaw, had stated that "the law is the law" and should be applied equally, even to Hitler.

He remembered that. He also remembered that he kinda liked Hitler.

"Say, talk to Millie Provis," Shaw said. "She was a town official during that whole thing."

Millie Provis, now 80 years old, and who admits, "My mind wanders sometimes," said maybe she can really help. "I'll talk to a couple of old-timers I know," she said, "and I'll get back to you. They're sure to know everything about Hitler."

That's the way it went. How can it be that in North Plains today Hitler is such a faint memory? Barely remembered? Why, it was Hitler who put North Plains on the map.

11   Linotype Dinosaur

Intro:

Just a couple of years before the *Sherman County Journal* newspaper became a century old, we went looking for the publisher. Not because the paper was about to turn 100. Oh, that was partly it. And too, the paper was even older by a few months, than the county that gave it its name. But it was more about how the Journal was printed that piqued our interest. Computers, you see, had taken over most newspaper production everywhere. But not in Moro, Oregon. No...no desktop creating here.

The Sherman County Journal building told you a lot, even before you went inside. It was a small weather-tortured, wood-frame structure, fronted by an elongated facade that still showed it had once been painted white.

Owner Dan Bartlett seemed determined to cling to the past, but he also seemed to be...well...hanging on by a thread. Newspaper publisher he might be in this tiny north-central Oregon town. But it was a sort of "moonlighting" job, with equipment that made him a dinosaur of publishers.

The working title for the story was "Hot Lead T-Rex." The title of record is "Linotype Dinosaur."

The Story:

Moro...a small town tucked into one of the folds of rolling wheat land of central Oregon. A place of some 320 population, and one newspaper. A newspaper nearly a century old. The *Sherman County Journal.*

And the Sherman County Journal has the distinction of being the only weekly newspaper in the state...some say the whole Northwest...still being cranked out on two old hot-lead typecasting machines.

Dan Bartlett is literally "moonlighting" here, although he owns the Sherman County Journal. Bartlett works full time for the Oregon Highway Department and spends his evenings trying to get the paper out in time for Thursday distribution. "Well, the dateline says 'Thursday,'" he declares, with a smile that you immediately understand means something other than Thursday, "but we try to get it out by Saturday." But then, if he misses the post office's Saturday deadline, the paper won't be delivered until Monday.

Some people say the old Linotype or Intertype machines will last forever. But Dan takes no chances. "We treat 'em pretty gentle." More than that, "I kinda hover over them to make sure nothing bad happens to them, cause the parts are irreplaceable anymore."

And in a time when most youngsters cut their teeth on computers, Dan's teenage son, Jess, is learning to operate Linotype.

Jess is fascinated by these dinosaurs of the newspaper business. "The machinery will run forever," he believes. He also has confidence that his dad can help them run forever.

The late Giles French, well-known Oregon rancher/publisher, once owned the newspaper. Dan's dad bought it from French. And Dan purchased the *Journal* from the people who bought it from Dan's father. "I worked for them," Dan explains, "and practically all the little money the paper made, they paid me in wages." So, the owners told him, "I might as well run it."

Income from the paper still won't support him, though. And that's the reason he works for the Highway Department. But when he retires from there in a few years, Dan says he can come to the newspaper and "really tend to business. Maybe even meet our Thursday deadline."

Postscript:

Sometimes when a man's luck runs bad, it runs all bad. In 1986, when we did the story about Dan Bartlett and the *Sherman County Journal*, he was a single dad. So, in addition to holding a full-time job and getting out the newspaper every week, he was raising three young sons, three, five, and eight years old. Plus, of course, he had the responsibility, as well, for the 'teen son, Jess, who was an apprentice at the paper. Well, all that was a handful, sure...but it wasn't bad luck.

But things did go "gunny bag" in the year of the *Journal's* centennial. That is: they went bad. They could not have been worse. While deep in preparation of the paper's Century Issue, Dan Bartlett was put out of commission.

A severe heart attack felled Bartlett as he hustled to meet the paper's 100th birthday in November of 1988. It was to be a big issue, absolutely, chronicling 100 years of the Journal's worth to the community, and the community's worth to the paper. Words and deeds past, words and deeds pointed at the future. Full of history and warm-hearted ads. That was to be the Centennial Issue of the *Sherman County Journal*. But now, all was in jeopardy.

Bartlett's heart attack turned into triple bypass surgery and a new valve. He was recovering, but he was down. Bad timing...bad luck. The paper was down, too. And worse, it appeared the Centennial Issue was doomed. But Dan had friends. Good friends.

One of them, Jack Healy, a former owner of the paper and for whom Bartlett once worked, pitched in. This, despite the fact, says Bartlett, that "Jack had a terrible allergy to printer's ink and his hands were raw all the time." Still, Healy got the *Journal* out for the next 14 weeks...over 3 months.

Next to help Bartlett's recuperation was retired newspaperman Robert McCain of Newberg, Oregon. McCain picked up the Centennial Issue pieces and worked them into the edition they were meant to be. All too late for the paper's 100th, but fortunately, in time for the Centennial Celebration of Sherman County in 1989. But barely.

The *Sherman County Journal* Centennial Issue, originally scheduled for publication in November 1988, was finally issued in September 1989. McCain saved the day with his computer. Yes...it was a desktop edition.

Yet, as the 21st century loomed, and there was talk of plugging every kid into computers, Dan Bartlett was still clinging to the past. Getting out his newspaper, "some months twice, some months just once." Plugged into his hot-lead machine. The Linotype.

And then, just as the second millennium turned, Dan Barlett died, leaving the past to others and the fate of the *Sherman County Journal* in doubt.

12   Autographs Broker

Intro:

George Washington, Brigham Young, Madonna, Neil Armstrong, and Marilyn Monroe all have something in common: their signatures are worth money.

And to a few entrepreneurs who can assess that worth, there's a living to be made, peddling historic and/or celebrity names... that is...selling autographs to collectors. Of course, that means anyone who wants to sell an autograph has to collect it first.

At Umpqua, Oregon, a wayside not much larger than a short name, an autograph collector named Ray Anthony brokered his and other people's celebrity signatures into money.

The working title for the story was "$ignature$." The title of record is "Autographs Broker."

The Story:

Ray Anthony of Umpqua, Oregon, could well be the envy of any devout autograph hound. He has over 12,000 autographs, signatures of well-known persons from both past and present. But Ray is not so much a collector as he is a salesman. You see, he collects because autographs are worth money; some of them are worth a lot of money. And they are his business, his way of making a living.

Call out a name. Ray probably has the signature. George Washington? Sure. Ray's price...$5,800. "This is a George Washington letter," says Anthony of the document on which the signature appears, "written by a secretary, but signed by him when he was commander of the armed forces." The date is December 16, 1780. The letter was to inform the recipient of a promotion in rank.

Richard Nixon's and Gerald Ford's signatures, written on a picture of the two taken on the day Nixon resigned the presidency, can be had for $1,250.

Ray just sold this Marilyn Monroe-autographed picture for $500. Marilyn's signature, he says, "is always 'hot.'"

He's priced a signed picture of John Lennon at $550. But if it were from the Beatles era of the 1960s, he might get over $20,000.

Already sold for nearly a thousand dollars is the signature of the "Lone Eagle," Charles Lindbergh. Not for his 1927 solo flight across the Atlantic. But for his name on the log that marked the beginning of the first commercial transcontinental flight, on which Lindbergh was the pilot.

On the other hand, the signature of Neil Armstrong, the first man on the moon, is worth just $65.

Extremely rare Mormon currency signed by Brigham Young and other church leaders in 1849 is a high-priced item: $5,800.

But the highest price Ray ever got for an autograph was for one of Abe Lincoln's. "I sold a document signed by Abraham Lincoln one time," he says, "for $7,500." To this date, that's it.

Ray points out that much of the value of a signature is based on the document on which it is written. Or the circumstances. For instance this check for $190.21 was signed by Rosalyn Carter, back in 1960, long before Jimmy started running for political offices that finally landed both of them in the White House. The thing that helps make this check unique is that it bounced. And we see it made it through on the second try.

Ray's wife, Linda, keeps track of the thousands of autographs; a computer, she says, is the "only way to keep the inventory continually updated." And Ray says authentication is another one of the hard parts of the business. That takes hours and hours of research. "I've just proved a 'Glen Miller,'" he says, "and I'm working on a 'James Hoffa.'" Four hundred others are waiting in the "in" bin.

Yet, in all his life, Ray insists, he has never gone up to a famous person and asked for an autograph. "It's true," he declares, "I'd be too embarrassed."

Postscript:

Ray Anthony has the same name as that of a popular orchestra leader, but there apparently is no other connection. The orchestra conductor was a look-alike for actor Cary Grant, but that didn't get much play either. The Umpqua, Oregon, Ray Anthony did not look like either Cary Grant or the music maker Ray Anthony. And so far as we know, did not have, nor want, his autograph unless it were worth some important money.

13   Spiders At Work

Intro:

One day, about 15 years ago, the spiders that persisted in connecting their webs from my fence to the house, across a narrow walkway, got my attention. Despite my repeated demolition of the strands, they were soon in place again, often in the same place, and sometimes within only a few hours.

I took to sighting through the webs at utility lines and saw similarity between the two works. Cameraman Don Stapleton saw it too. We added a sprightly piano to the video and narration, which made it seem as if the spiders were working even faster.

The working title was "Study of the In Common Link Between Arachnids and Humans." The title of record is "Spiders at Work."

The Story:

Spiders, like men, are fond of running lines everywhere. Some of the results are criss-crosses of seeming disorder. Others, patterns of perfect organization.

Humans and spiders have another thing in common: they are not particularly fond of each other. But the spider that sent Miss Muffet scurrying away whey-faced probably had not the slightest intention of scaring her. More likely, it was looking for a place to fix an anchor line. To a spider a tuffet might seem to be as good a place as any.

A lot of people don't study spiders as I do. Those are the people who can tell you what they're up to, and call them by name. All I know is they're plenty busy most of the time. But particularly busy now, in the fall.

And I've done some experiments. And, thereby, I've learned a broken web can be repaired, or even replaced, overnight. And I've noticed that some spiders seem to be acutely aware of their surroundings. Even to the extent that spiders in the Mima Mounds of Washington State build webs that look like mounds. And that some spiders help in the harvest. They eat up bugs that might eat up the harvest.

And I don't know if it's an old wives' tale or not, but most spiders are said to have at least a little poison in their system. That's pretty common in men too, you know. Yet, we live with each other. So, I guess we can live with spiders. I know I can.

As long as they stay out of the house.

Postscript:

A lot of people kill spiders. But none of the people I know who kill spiders are women. Two reasons: one is that some women are so afraid of spiders they won't go anywhere near one, even to squash it. The other is that some other women revere spiders and will not let anyone mash them. I'm not sure why that is, but it may be a holdover from the times when spiders had to be alive, you know, when they went into a witch's brew.

So, if you have a woman in the house who runs from spiders, you are an executioner. The spider gets squished on orders of "squish it, squish it!" On the other hand, if she insists that a spider in the house be captured alive in a glass and put outside, "because spiders do so many good things," we're wary. She may do it herself, but it's more likely you have to do it.

And any woman who likes spiders tells you there are no more spiders around than are necessary.

If that's true, it's a thing spiders have over people. I've never heard anybody, woman or man, say there are no more people around than are necessary.

14   Nashville Connection

Intro:

It's a long, long road between Nashville, Oregon, and Nashville, Tennessee. But a young Oregon singer was determined to travel that route to the Grand Ole Opry. The dream was to follow in the footsteps of the likes of Patsy Cline and Hank Williams and win fame alongside performers like Reba McIntyre and George Jones. Maybe even fill somebody's shoes.

The story of Shannon O'Donnell began as a rumbling logging truck rolled through the quaint village of Nashville, Oregon; that rumble slowly became intertwined with the sound of music. A country/western band? Yes...and then a voice, a pretty voice, sadly proclaiming that God had no hand in making honky-tonk angels.

The working title for the 1985 story was "Shannon's Two Nashvilles." The title of record is "Nashville Connection."

The Story:

Nashville, Oregon...where there used to be a post office; where there used to be a store; where they used to count the population. A crossroads, named not for the Tennessee city of Grand Ole Opry fame, but for an English lawyer, Wallis

Nash, who helped found one of Oregon's large colleges. But not in Nashville. Nash was also instrumental in pushing the railroad through here.

A granite marker indicates that, perhaps, the place should have been named for James Hamar, the first settler on this spot. It wasn't. But Hamar's homestead was what is now Nashville.

So it seems there is no connection between Nashville, Oregon, and Nashville, Tennessee...except the name. So, wouldn't it be the wildest of fantasies to imagine there is a country/western singer here, who wants to make it big at the Grand Ole Opry there?

"It wasn't God who made honky-tonk angels," sings the pretty voice, the lyrics flowing through the lips of a becoming face, on which freckles race back and forth from cheek to cheek across the bridge of the nose. A face framed by...is it red, or reddish, hair?

Shannon O'Donnell...18-year-old high school senior...has that dream; the Grand Ole Opry. Right now she sings mostly at pizza parlors and Grange halls and in rehearsals with her dad and his band. Shannon knows it's a rough road to Nashville, Tennessee.

"We entered a country music contest," she says. "And we didn't win, but it didn't bother me much." It was Shannon's first performance in a bar and "I had a blast." A good time, she means...not a drink. "And I just thought we'd win next time, next time I'll do it."

Shannon holds several jobs to earn money now. One of them is feeding a neighbor's horses and cleaning out stalls. She says she'll also get a college degree before heading out for Nashville. "I'll major in something I can make money at," she says, "so I can fall back on something if I don't make it in Nashville."

The nice voice with the freckled schoolgirl face polishes off Honky-Tonk Angels. "...That has caused many a good girl to go wrong." Followed by a dazzling smile, filled with even white teeth.

Shannon O'Donnell. Right now in Nashville...Oregon.

Postscript:

The winters in Jackson Hole, Wyoming, are cold! The summers are hot! But the scenery in this western valley is spectacular. Grand mountain ranges...the Tetons, Wind River, Gros Ventre surround Jackson Hole, much like a circle of wagons against Indian attack. But the mountains are so beautiful they are no defense for the small town of Jackson sitting on the sagebrush valley floor. Instead they compel tourists and sports fans alike to crowd in, in any season. The rugged circle is a playground, especially in winter.

It is here that Shannon O'Donnell of Nashville, Oregon, works in a Jackson bank.

No fame? No fortune? No Grand Ole Opry?

Shannon did get in two-and-a-half years of study in animal science at Oregon State University. But with a break in the middle. "I took courses until I ran out of money," she says. "Then I left school and drove 18-wheelers for awhile to earn enough money to go back."

But other things happened to dampen Shannon's resolve

to become a country/western music star. She met in Newport, Oregon, with an important record producer, a woman, who indicated accepting some sexual passes is as necessary as a good voice to getting ahead. "I didn't like the idea of being 'touched' for business' sake," Shannon declared.

"That possibility repulsed me. But looking back, I was just out of high school and pretty naive." Now she knows the producer was wrong; it's not required that one sleep one's way to the top.

Another thing...Shannon dislikes the turn country/western music has taken in recent years. "It isn't country music, it isn't western music. What passes for country/western today is country rock. I don't care for it."

And yet another thing: "Along the way I became a born-again Christian," explains Shannon. "And when I began to sing for the Lord, the Grand Ole Opry didn't seem so important."

A few years ago she moved to Jackson Hole, where she has friends, and took the bank job. But one of those friends recently opened the door to new opportunity. "Another way to use my voice for the Lord," Shannon says.

The friend got a record producer interested in Shannon's voice. Gary Sadler, songwriter for Hosanna Integrity Music, flew her to his studios, and in a four-day session Shannon recorded ten Gospel songs...within a stone's throw of the Grand Ole Opry Hall.

Yes. Right there...in...Nashville, Tennessee!

"It was not for the purpose of building a career for Shannon O'Donnell," declares Shannon. "Dubs of those tapes will go into the service of the Lord."

But it was fun to tour Nashville and "thrilling to see the hall, at last."

15   Pioneer Grave

"Missis Butts dyed this day," wrote Oregon Trail pioneer Samuel Parker in his diary on October 2, 1845, at the Deschutes River crossing. It was not a good time to die, especially now when succor at The Dalles Mission on the Columbia River was less than a week's travel away. Catherine Butts, mother of seven, would never see the "Promised Land" of the Oregon Territory's lush Willamette Valley. She was one of perhaps 30 pioneers who died on the trek of the Meek Cutoff, the awful ordeal of the Lost Wagon Train.

On October 5, after crossing the Deschutes, Parker wrote: "...heare we beried missis Butts and 3 more."

Nearly a century and a half later, photog Mike Slowik and I joined a latter-day caravan, to do a story on the dedication of "Missis Butts's" grave.

The working title for the story was "Lost Wagon Train Grave." The title of record is "Pioneer Grave."

The Story:

Windswept, lonely, remote is the grave of Catherine Bonnett Butts, one of the thousands of emigrants who perished on the Oregon Trail, hastily buried in the rocky

93

ground, left to history.

The early part of Mrs. Butts's trek West probably matched scenes like these along the Oregon Trail:

Fort Kearny in present-day central Nebraska.

Approaching Chimney Rock in western Nebraska.

Three Island crossing of the Snake River in Idaho.

And now, spread out in a caravan reminiscent of a wagon train, some 50 of Catherine Butts's descendants and historians have come to Tygh Valley, Oregon, to dedicate her grave...143 years after her death on the trail in 1845.

The five-mile trek, along a muddy track, presents its own difficulties. And maybe something like pioneers of the Oregon Trail, some abandon their vehicles in favor of walking, or hitching rides aboard sturdier rigs. But all trudge past a nearby relic ranch, and finally arrive at the pioneer grave.

Dick Ackerman of the Oregon/California Trails Association states the purpose. "We are here today to dedicate this grave site to Catherine Bonnett Butts and three other unknown pioneers."

We learn that Mrs. Butts and other members of her party had the misfortune to be led by Stephen Meek, he of the infamous Meek's Cutoff to the Willamette Valley. The Meek Cutoff: an untried, untraced route, along which the wagon train got lost, then wandered, split up, and finally headed north toward The Dalles.

The wagons had just reached the Deschutes River, not far from that goal, when Catherine Butts died.

Most of her descendants, from the oldest to the

youngest, already know all that. One of them, David Sheelar, says, "Her history is our history, part of our tradition. We're really proud of that."

Part of that tradition is that the lost wagon train stumbled upon a "mother lode" of gold. And the legend built on that supposed find refers to the place as the Blue Bucket Mine...which to this day also remains lost.

But author Lowell Tiller, who wrote a book about the train, says all that gold fever was based on a solitary nugget found by one wagon member, Daniel Herren.

"Daniel wrote to his granddaughter and said he found a piece of gold about the size of a man's thumb," declares Tiller. "And from that the legend has grown."

And more important, as pointed out here today, the pioneers came to settle, to raise crops and families. And in doing that, they played a major role in stretching the nation from the Atlantic to the Pacific. That is the heritage most remembered here today, at the grave of Catherine Bonnett Butts.

"...and 3 more."

Postscript:

In their book _Terrible Trail: the Meek Cutoff, 1845_, co-authors Lowell Tiller and Keith Clark pieced together the entire route of the Lost Wagon Train and the story of its horrible suffering. They also narrowed the area of search for the gold discovery, even suggesting a zone where prospectors might want to look. That was over 30 years ago. To date, no one has rediscovered the Blue Bucket Mine.

Also, Stephen Meek is not to be confused with his younger brother Joe Meek, who made his mark, too, as detailed in another chapter of this book.

16   Dam Women

Intro:

Women have been pretty certain all along they could do most jobs. Not only those jobs they've traditionally done, but those traditionally done by men as well. But it has not been easy for women to break into the masculine job ranks. Even tougher to obtain equal pay and benefits and respect.

In this latest skirmish in the battle of the sexes, men have either hindered the fight, or dodged it. Some men, to their credit...or discredit...depending on whom one considers to be the enemy, have actually helped women get "men's jobs."

Women have always known as well as men how to fight dirty. But in the roughhouse of job hunting, they absolutely showed no mercy. First, they set in motion the Equal Rights Amendment for the distaff. Then they got themselves declared a minority, no small accomplishment since women are, roughly, half the population.

But, of course, we knew what they meant: let's end this discrimination and get on with the work.

So, a couple of decades ago we reported about the "breakthrough" women made in construction crafts on a major building project on the Columbia River.

The working title for the story was "Damn Women."

The title of record is "Dam Women."

The Story:

The lady's name is Flo Hedges. And while she's proved she's no "cream puff," still many people would think of her as being out of place: perched as she is, high in the cab of this triple-7...a gargantuan dump truck.

Flo is part of the crew that's building a second power-house at Bonneville Dam on the Columbia River. She wheels this big rig back and forth, between tailrace excavation and spoils dump site a couple of miles away, about six times an hour. The livelong day. She nailed down the job, after being urged on by her husband. She likes it. And she's good at it.

But Flo is only one of about 60 women who have jobs on the powerhouse construction...through the "affirmative action program" of the joint contractors. Most are apprentices. But all are blazing trails into construction craft unions: the teamsters, ironworkers, cement finishers, carpenters, operating engineers...and yes...laborers.

And, whatever the reasons they've chosen this rugged work, highest on the list is that the pay is good.

Rosie, the riveter, faded away at the end of World War II. But Diane Rafanan, a welder, is helping the resurgence of women in such jobs. Diane works side-by-side with, and is learning from, Mike Ewing. Mike says he believes women on such jobs are here to stay.

"It's the first time I've ever worked with a woman ironworker," says Ewing. "But I think it'll work out, there'll be more of 'em all the time."

But Diane qualified that. She says it will take special women. "The majority of women who try this are just not going to last," she says. "The work is hard, strenuous and you have to do equally what everyone else does. You're not going to be a housewife one day and jump into this kind of work the next. For most it'll be too hard for them."

The carpentry shop, however, is liberally laced with females. Six, in all. Among them: Jane Rondthaler, who says she is here because she reached a "dead end" after nine years as a school teacher. She says she eagerly jumped in when she learned a woman "with three grown kids could still get an apprenticeship."

And then there's Phyllis Paulino of Vancouver, Washington, who's getting practical experience to help build her own home. "I'd like to stick with it for the whole program," Phyllis states. "And eventually, I'd like to get into residential construction and solar heating."

Clay Vestal, business manager for the contractor, says despite the inroads made by women on the dam job, there's room for more to fill the affirmative action goal. "I think the biggest reason for not matching the goal," reasons Vestal, "is lack of previous exposure by women to the construction industry and this type of work."

So, more and more women could be filling jobs such as those held by Donna Bunk and Ada Hoffman, mechanics...helping to keep machinery running and rolling. And that of Kathy Rivera, who...may all the saints preserve us...is a cement finisher.

"I'm not a women's libber," Kathy disclaims. "But I prefer to do this hard construction work for good money, than an office job for practically no money."

"It's a man's world" is a cry not often heard here these days. But, Clay Vestal insists that women after jobs at Bonneville "will have to 'cut the mustard.'" If they can do the jobs, he explains, just fine. But if they can't, "we run them off as fast as we do any man who can't 'cut it.'"

Postscript:

Women's persistence has paid off. Everywhere you look today, women have jobs. Formerly men's jobs. But it would be inaccurate to identify almost any work now as either men's or women's. That's how far the women's battle for equality in job opportunity has taken them. And thus, us.

Sure, there's more work to be done. Women are not satisfied. And probably won't be until a time when they perceive they have reached the goal of equality. When that will be is anybody's guess.

One thing is certain. There is at least one job women cannot do. There is not a woman alive who can take out the garbage. That, women concede...no, insist...is a man's job.

17   Kitty Hall

Intro:

The estate planning was nearly "purrfect." At least
that's the way it seemed in the case of an heiress in the tiny
town of Tangent, Oregon. She was set for life. She would
have no more worries than when her patron, John Bass, was
alive. He owned the property, a big white house, a big red
barn, a grove of oak trees, and over three acres of land. And
when he died, Bass left it all to her...his significant com-
panion.

To Kitty Kat.

The working title for the story was "Fat Cat." The title
of record is "Kitty Hall."

The Story:

John Bass was 82 years old when he died, Kitty Kat was
about nine, so in terms of human age she was then something like 63 years old. No wonder Bass took care to see
that Kitty Kat would be provided for. There was an execu-
tor to look after the legal end of the estate, of course, like
there is in so many things where a lawyer is required. And
a caretaker, a longtime friend of Bass's, who would take
care of the property and Miss Kitty.

Bass, to his great credit, realized that, in time, Kitty Kat was bound to lose all nine of her lives. If she got run over, they would all be gone in one fell swoop. And one could only guess how many she had already lost by not landing on her feet, things like that.

However, if she lived a normal life, he must have reasoned, she would lose them only sporadically, maybe no more than one at a time. She could live a long time. So he planned to make all the rest of her lives as comfortable as possible.

The estate was valued at around $250,000. A lot of comfort for a cat. And then when she died, stipulated Bass, she was to be buried on the grounds, with a headstone inscribed with her name, Kitty Kat, and the tribute "A True Friend."

The will stated she was to live in the big, white house. And as reason would have it, that meant she could also hunt mice in the barn, and climb the trees if she wanted to.

Yes, "purrfect."

Yet, something was missing...or someone. Not Dale Clark, the sworn caretaker. He took care of her fine. He fed her, watered her, saw she got her exercise, petted her. He also was her press agent, telling things to television and newspaper reporters he thought she might want them to know. But he also had the grounds to keep up, and besides he lived in a mobile home clear over on the other edge of the land. He was good company, but he was a servant. Besides, he had a big dog.

But then, a need of the City of Tangent for an expanded seat of government...that is, more space...promised to cure Kitty's loneliness. You see, Bass's will also stipulated that when Kitty died, the house would go the city for use as a historical site. But could Tangent's government and Kitty Kat share the huge house ahead of time, make it the City Hall?

Yes they could, in the opinion of estate attorney Roger Reid, who seemed to reflect the spirit of the will. And so it happened that the cat's house became Kitty Hall.

In new chambers the city council tackled such knotty problems as a new sewer system, a nuisance petition, the budget...as Kitty Kat circulated around the room, like she was flaunting her ownership of the place. But council members thought she was more likely lobbying for strokes, and so rubbed her fur, the right way. She often rested on backs of chairs, occupied by council members, or was underfoot.

During the meetings, Kitty Kat sometimes dozed, as the elderly are prone to do. But most of the time she was attentive. All of which seemed to help, rather than hinder, council decisions. It was an exchange, a quid pro quo.

But the city did have a slight problem. It seems that to be in the building, the city had to match the estate fund for expenses. That is, share the utility bills. And sometimes the city was slow to scratch up the money. But it did. The city was also expected to provide insurance for its use of the building. It did. It was loose, but it was working.

But a half-dozen years later, the deal soured. The house that Kitty Kat inherited needed a new furnace. Kitty's attorney, that same Roger Reid, thought the city should share the $5,000 cost for the replacement. The city refused to help.

The scat hit the fan. Reid, on the behalf of Kitty,

although it is doubtful Kitty was either consulted about or sanctioned the action, evicted the council. City government returned to its former quarters at the town's community hall. Kitty Kat, caught in the middle, took the heat. "Cat evicts city council," the headlines accused.

Kitty returned to being pretty much alone. In addition, now being denied access to the barn where she used to run down mice, she probably contemplated hunting birds to get her exercise. But the trees were so tall, and she was so old, that it would have been nice if there had been ground-level bird feeders to make it easier. But no.

Three years later Kitty Kat was dead, at the age of 140, or about 20 in feline years. She was laid to rest in a miniature crypt beneath a little marker that does say "Kitty Kat, A True Friend." A larger slab of marble, in the same rock-bordered enclosure, identifies the place as the John Bass farm.

Postscript:

Now, of course, the city has inherited the property, owns it. It must be maintained as a historic place. The town of just 340 people must now think big. Will the big, white house again become City Hall? Or will it become a place of bed and breakfast?

More likely, indicates a blue-ribbon committee, the house and grounds will be designated as a community hall and park for weddings, receptions, reunions, and picnics...for a fee.

In that way "Kitty Hall" will be a self-supporting historic place.

18   Erector Set Bridges

Intro:

Some people may wonder why so many buildings and bridges and things like Ferris wheels and roller coasters look like they were made by children. It might be because of the influence of an Oregon native who invented a toy called the Erector Set; a toy that lasted for most of the 20th century.

A.C. Gilbert was the first to admit his toy was fashioned on real buildings and bridges and such. But today, long after his death, there are professional builders who indicate they, in turn, were inspired by Erector Sets.

The working title for the story in 1984 was "Erection Sets." The title of record is "Erector Set Bridges."

The Story:

First, let's take a look at Erector Sets. And right we should. A.C. Gilbert, who invented the Erector Set, was born right here in Oregon...Salem. Gilbert died in 1961, following a lifetime chock-full of accomplishments. He won a gold medal in the 1908 Olympic Games in London, in what was then called "pole jumping" by the British, but "pole vaulting" by nearly everybody else.

Gilbert's next big jump was into inventing, manufacturing, and marketing toys. Among them: chemistry sets, magic kits, woodworking kits, the American Flyer trains. And the Erector Set.

The collection of Gilbert's toys, here at the Mission Mill in Salem, belongs to Bill Charnholm and is on display to mark the 100th anniversary of Gilbert's birth. Charnholm says Gilbert put his mark on millions of children's lives in a positive way.

"It's the kind of toy that makes kids think," says Charnholm. "The kind of toy that inspires them to invent new toys with it."

For example, take the Marquam Bridge, here in Portland. When it was built in the 1960s, there were some people who said it looked like it was made from a giant Erector Set. But the man in charge of that project at the time doesn't take that as an insult.

Ivan Merchant declares, "No way...in no way do I take that as an insult." He explains that both the Marquam Bridge and an Erector Set bridge are "truss bridges," constructed on sound engineering rules. "They are much the same."

Some other bridges of the kind include the Interstate 5 (I-5) Bridge between Portland and Vancouver and the Astoria Bridge at the mouth of the Columbia River. There are many others. But Merchant points out the truth that truss bridges came long before the Erector Set.

But during World War II, an Erector Set was used for scale model design of the Bailey Bridge. Most Northwesterners will remember it was a Bailey Bridge that was used to reconnect the Spirit Lake Highway after Mount St. Helens mudflows wiped out bridges on the Toutle River.

But is there an Erector Set connection with bridge builders? The current Oregon bridge design engineer Walter Hart has a staff of 40 bridge designers. So we put the question to him. Is there?

"That's an interesting question," says Hart. "And when you asked me to do the survey, I had no idea I'd be so surprised by the results." The fact is, according to Hart, that "over half of the design engineers had Erector Sets when they were youngsters."

So there. But...well...sure, building really big bridges isn't child's play. But let's hope it's fun.

Postscript:

The pole-vaulting technique invented by A.C. Gilbert and with which he set a world's record in the U.S. Olympic trials in 1908 was disallowed at the Olympics in London. The technique involved digging a hole for a "cup" or "box" in which to plant the end of the pole as the vaulter approached the bar. The method was really beginning to catch on with other pole vaulters, too. (It is the same technique used by all vaulters today.) But the British ruled the system "illegal," forcing Gilbert to use the traditional spiked pole.

Gilbert won the gold anyway, but the ban ruined his chances of breaking his own world record.

In 1989 A.C. Gilbert was honored by his hometown in a

way befitting his contribution to kids of the country. A fine old Victorian house, perhaps one much like the home in which Gilbert spent the first years of his life in Salem, was dedicated as the Gilbert House Children's Museum.

At the time, college surveys reinforced my years-earlier poll which counted Erector Set owners among Oregon's bridge designers. Martin Morris, then the museum's director, said many of the nation's "brightest minds developed with Gilbert toys." Engineering students, pre-med students, chemistry students. In fact, according to Morris, "A majority of them had grown up with both Erector Sets and chemistry sets" and a variety of Gilbert-produced toys.

The museum devoted a room exclusively to Gilbert family history, and to Alfred Carlton "A.C." Gilbert's contribution to generations of science-minded youngsters.

But Gilbert made his mark in other ways. He popularized the coffee break for employees, gave them paid vacations and maternity leave. And not all of his inventions were kid stuff. He came up with versions of food processors and mini-vacuum cleaners and what many of us may think was his greatest invention, one he first produced in the 1920s...the hand-held hair dryer.

And don't think that Erector Sets are strictly museum pieces. They are history, it's true. And for a time there, following Gilbert's death and a sequence of company takeovers, it appeared Erector would die.

But in recent years Maccano company acquired the worldwide license of the Erector name, and kids in the last of the 20th Century played with new Erector Sets. Millions of them.

19   Rotten Sneakers

Intro:

Probably everyone in America owns at least one pair of beat-up old tennis shoes; that is...worn-out sneakers. So it seemed promoters of a "rotten sneakers" contest in Lincoln City, Oregon, had a great idea.

Until the day of the competition.

Only one contestant showed up. A little boy, wearing a pair of shoes that fit every category of the event. They were worn and ragged and smelly, as rotten sneakers should be. They had ragged holes scattered mostly where toes showed through and streaks of something here and there. They were grungy; they qualified, beyond doubt. And they were topped off by a cute kid with a slightly runny nose.

The contest went forward, despite the fact...or perhaps because of the fact...that only one small child had the guts to enter the shoes to which he had given such a licking, but were still kicking.

The working title for the story was "Something's Rotten In Lincoln City." The title of record is "Rotten Sneakers."

The Story:

At first glance you'd think everybody wants into the competition. And what better source of sneakers is there than a group of kids? There must be 30, 40 youngsters here. All wearing tennis shoes. Looks like the Lincoln City Community Center's "Rotten Sneakers" contest is off to a great start.

But no. These first and second-graders from Cloverdale, Oregon, came here to swim in the center's pool. And now they're on their way home, taking their sneakers with them.

As it turns out, only one contestant turns up: seven-year-old Ammon Poage of Otis Junction. His mom, Linda, younger sister, Trish, and baby brother, Andy, have come to cheer him on.

It looks like this lone competitor...all right, if you insist...this sole competitor, should cop every ribbon in the place. There must be 15 to 20 categories, ranging from "Genuinely Worn" to "Grungiest" to "Rubber Rot" to "Fungus Among Us."

But incredibly, the judges see fit to award Ammon only one first-place ribbon...for "Air-conditioned Toes."

It seems the rules allow "absentia" contestants who simply left their shoes here. That's right: no-shows are allowed to show their shoes. One pair of these won four blue ribbons, not the least of which was for "grungiest."

The "absent" owner, Hank Knight, was also handy for an interview because he is the center's pool manager. No conflict of interest here, apparently. The contest is open to everyone.

"Shucks, I was surprised as anybody, that I won so many ribbons," laughs Hank. "I thought if I won anything it would be the 'Least Likely to Last' category."

And Ammon Poage, the one-and-only walk-in, walk-right-up contestant, was tickled with his prize, too. "I think I'll put this ribbon on my wall, and I hope I'll get one like it when I go to wrestling."

I'm wearing sneakers, too. They're about ten years old and are pretty rotten. They've had a lot of wear, as anyone can tell. And since the rules for the contest are so loose, I'm tempted to jump in. But I see they don't have a category for shoes that have "Come the Farthest."

Postscript:

Ammon Poage must be a young man, an adult, by now. I sometimes wonder if he sometimes wonders about why his shoes didn't win four blue ribbons. They were certainly worthy enough.

He was too young to learn the lesson I did that day: that even blue ribbons can seem to be management perks, even in an innocent fun contest. Even though Ammon was pleased with his single first-place ribbon, he should have had more. It would have been a lot nicer to have awarded him extra "Rotten Sneakers" prizes.

I doubt that he thinks like that. But I do. I might not think like that if I were a seven-year-old boy.

20   Sasquatch

Intro:

Everybody was jumping on the Bigfoot bandwagon. So, perhaps, it was inevitable that someone in the federal government would become a friend. In December of 1977, when most people were polishing up their belief in Santa Claus, the associate director of the U.S. Fish and Wildlife Service, Keith Schreiner, announced the National Guard would be called out to protect Bigfoot, if Bigfoot were real.

It was a plan so perfect that Bigfoot himself might have helped draft it, while sharing an eggnog with Schreiner.

The plan was that any Bigfoot caught was to be considered genuine, and would be placed on the endangered species list. And thus, must be protected by the National Guard.

But the feds were really late. Nearly a decade late. Earlier, people in Stevenson, Washington had seen the need to safeguard Bigfoot, a.k.a. Sasquatch. They did it with rule of law. An ordinance.

The working title for the story was "Bigfoot." The title of record is "Sasquatch."

The Story:

If there's one thing you don't do in Skamania County, Washington, it's harm a Bigfoot. You know, the legendary creature the Indians call Sasquatch, which means the same thing...Bigfoot.

Not that people have all that much opportunity to maim or kill a Bigfoot, because the critters make themselves pretty scarce, being anti-social because they're shy.

But a flurry of Bigfoot sightings back in 1969 prompted a movement to legislate compassion for him. One of the leaders in the "let's protect Sasquatch" crusade was Roy Craft, publisher of the Stevenson newspaper. Craft, once a publicist for both Marilyn Monroe and Elvis Presley, now had the task of whipping up public support for a beast only a few persons had seen—maybe had seen.

But Craft carefully chronicled the "sightings" episodes: Bigfoot jumped out of the fog in front of a "stone sober" motorist near Beacon Rock on the Columbia River; there were Sasquatch tracks in the snow within a few miles of the town of Carson, Washington; the sheriff's office made plaster casts of huge footprints in another location; a couple of backpackers followed a trail of giant tracks and swore they belonged to Bigfoot, although they didn't see a Bigfoot. Things like that.

Craft was even moved to issue a special edition of his weekly newspaper to help readers keep track of Sasquatch. Craft's old knack for promoting movie stars certainly assisted in boosting Bigfoot's image and encouraging county officials to protect him with a statute.

A short time later, Skamania County passed such an edict. No one, it said, would be allowed to "wantonly slay" a Bigfoot.

"It was not only for the protection of Bigfoot," said Craft, "but for the protection of the general public, as well." That's because rumors circulated that Bigfoot was worth $3 million, dead or alive.

"That brought an influx of hunters with big rifles," Craft declared. "And we didn't want some tourist, bent down to pick a huckleberry, to be mistaken for Bigfoot and blown away."

Authorities, including the county attorney, Robert Leick, figured it would be highly unlikely that any Bigfoot would attack a human. But if such an event did occur and the human were forced to kill the creature, the killer could "probably plead self-defense."

So, no matter what happens elsewhere in the northwest, Bigfoot will always be safe in Skamania County.

And Roy Craft states a truth. "Even if you don't believe in Bigfoot, you're always on the lookout for him."

Postscript:

I take a grain of salt with every Sasquatch story. Still, I always remember Roger Patterson, who shot footage of a creature in northern California that matched the image of descriptions of Bigfoot, and became the standard by which the ape creature is described by people who claim to have spotted him.

Patterson was an earnest young rodeo performer who brought his film to our newsroom in the mid-1960s, right after a "pack-trip encounter with Bigfoot." The footage showed a huge, hairy brute, perhaps seven feet tall, strolling in ground-gobbling strides, away from the camera. At one point, the creature hesitates and turns its face full to Patterson, and then is obscured by forest.

We did a story, carefully pointing out that while the film and Patterson's account were mighty intriguing, we had no way of corroborating either. That film clip has been used numerous times, in an assortment of Bigfoot stories, including a documentary by Patterson himself. To date, no one has proven it to be a hoax.

On the other hand, there are reasons to retain skepticism about Bigfoot. Most have to do with people who are avid believers, but who have strange ways of convincing others about the existence of Sasquatch.

For example: At a hearing in Skamania County years later to update the Bigfoot ordinance, a solemn witness with scientific bearing stated there were "two kinds of Sasquatches." The person drew a chalk line dividing a blackboard in two and wrote at the top of one section: "Hairy Sasquatch." At the top of the other: "Hairless Sasquatch."

It was news to everybody that there were Bigfoots without hair. But they took the revelation in good spirit, some rolling their eyes upward in their sockets, others choking off laughs.

Another Bigfoot advocate testified that he had "burst

into Bigfoot's bedroom," the bedroom being a small area of crushed brambles in the woods.

"I came within minutes of catching Sasquatch at home," he said. How did he know that? "Because I could smell his terrible body odor."

And, over time, there have been confessions by a few people who said they made false Bigfoot tracks. And other persons who claimed it was they who set off the ape creature legend on Mount St. Helens.

Then there's the fact that some people just will not take Bigfoot seriously. There's the 1977 Oregon Legislature, for example. A bill to protect Bigfoot was introduced in the House of Representatives. The House treated the measure with good humor, but not as though it was so much foofaraw, and passed it.

In contrast, it failed to get by the Senate. In fact, in the opinion of long-time serious Bigfoot researcher Peter Byrne, the Senate "made a joke" of the measure.

Sometimes, believers such as Byrne are as elusive as Bigfoot himself. We went to Byrne's Bigfoot museum in The Dalles, Oregon, hoping to photograph plaster foot casts, supposedly belonging to Bigfoot. But Byrne was off in Nepal, chasing after that country's equivalent to Bigfoot...the Abominable Snowman...Yeti.

Remember that U.S. Fish and Wildlife official, Keith Schreiner? Well, at the time he stated he was inclined to protect Bigfoot he also reminded us that if a Sasquatch should be captured, it would not be the first time a new species was discovered. He pointed out that the gorilla and giant panda were only legends until their existence was finally confirmed as fact in the late 19th century.

But in the early 21st century, Bigfoot is still only legend. And while there have been any number of reasons to call out the National Guard, including participation in the Persian Gulf War, the Guard is still waiting for the call to guard Bigfoot.

21   Meek Graffiti

Intro:

Mountain man Joe Meek made a big mark on Oregon history. Antithesis to his name, Meek was anything but weak or humble. Meek was a frontiersman, an explorer, a fur trapper, sometimes in the company of other explorers and trappers and his Nez Perce wife. But often alone. He was wilderness-rough-and-tumble. He once was a lawman.

But there is evidence along the way he made his mark in another way. He apparently left some frontier graffiti that, if done today, could get him in trouble.

The working title for the story was "Meek Doodling." The title of record is "Meek Graffiti."

The Story:

Evidence of human inhabitants at Willamette Falls pre-dates mountain man Joe Meek by thousands of years. Black Point at the falls at Oregon City, Oregon, contains Indian petroglyphs, etched so deep they've survived hundreds, perhaps thousands, of years.

"This particular site is a wealth of prehistory peoples," according to cultural artist Greg Bettis, who has made a career out of recording, drawing, and painting such symbols. "Many of these rock carvings," he says, "can be interpreted to mean a territorial boundary."

It was while searching for Indian carvings at the falls that Greg made another exciting discovery. Scratched into the face of the cliff is the name of Joe Meek, dated 1841.

Could this be the Joe Meek—the mountain man, the trapper, the first sheriff of the territory—the same Joe Meek who later hanged five Indians connected with the Whitman massacre?

Greg showed us the spot, but as he led us to the place, it became abundantly clear why the Meek carving, if it is that of Meek, is so unknown. Most of the time the site is under water.

During periods of high water, and standing on the viewpoint that overlooks this area, and seeing the raging torrent, it's difficult to imagine that during low water, one can actually stand here in the main chute. Not far from the chute is Joe Meek's name.

But during low water there are restrictions, too. Private industry, the Oregon Fish and Wildlife Department, and the Clackamas County River Patrol discourage trespassing. But even with their permission, it takes a good deal of rock climbing to see Meek's handiwork.

But is it Meek's handiwork? Greg Bettis believes it is authentic. And was probably chiseled with his knife. Meek is known to have signed on as a pilot and assistant with the party of Lieutenant Charles Wilkes, who explored the Cowlitz and Willamette Rivers in 1841.

"We know that Wilkes was here," states Bettis. "We know that Meek was with Wilkes. We know it was June 1841. We assume it was a time of low water. We believe it was Joe Meek who etched his name here."

Anyone carving his name on these rocks today would be called a vandal. And even now, Joe Meek's signature can be considered frontier graffiti. But, of course, he was on a government-santioned expedition; and then there's the passage of time, so it is now an important historic marker.

At Willamette Falls at Oregon City.

Postscript:

In another place at another time, somewhere in Oregon, the blast of a train whistle ricochets off the cliffs of the Columbia River Gorge. Within sight and sound of this modern machinery is another site of prehistoric man. A location where centuries ago...perhaps millennia ago...stood an ancient village.

It is spots like this that Greg Bettis, who took us to the Meek site, continues his consuming quest of documenting rock carvings and paintings, petroglyphs and pictographs...Indian art, believed to have been "a form of spiritual communication."

Bettis has hiked thousands of miles in canyons in areas of Arizona, Utah, Oregon, and Washington, to record all he finds in minutely detailed drawings of his own.

"I'm not an expert, such as an archaeologist," says the tall, rangy cultural artist. "My expertise is merely to record rock art. And that, in itself, is a difficult and challenging job."

Reservoirs of Columbia River Dams have drowned

many such sites. But some of the ancient art has been saved. A petroglyph gallery at The Dalles Dam is evidence of such preservation. The carvings were chiseled out in chunks as the dam was being built in the 1950s. Even here Greg finds material for his research.

But throughout the region it is at little-known places, many on private property, that Greg finds what he calls "pristine" sites—spots that have escaped spray-can vandals. And what Greg calls "erosion" caused by pattern rubbing.

The art in these special places was not art for art's sake, but had extraordinary meaning. They were spiritual symbols, it's believed, but which now resist giving up exact insight. It is enough for Greg Bettis that he recognizes the figures are well-executed in "design, movement, and containment." And are "almost contemporary in form."

With that in mind, Greg replicates some of his drawings of them as framed prints...as part of his own art.

22   Celilo Drain Plan

Intro:

A couple of years before Washington State was to celebrate its centennial, some residents of the state's Klickitat County, along the Columbia River, said they knew just what was needed for the state to make a really big splash on its 100th birthday.

Drain Celilo Lake behind The Dalles Dam! And thereby expose the ancient Indian fishing grounds, Celilo Falls, which itself went down the drain when flooded out by the dam reservoir.

A brainstorm it was, appreciated by nearly everyone and applauded by many. But supported by only a few. After all, Celilo Lake was a key element in the Columbia "mechanical river" system: a series of dams and reservoirs whose power generation lit up a vast region, irrigated tens of thousands of acres and helped make Clarkston/Lewiston, Idaho, on the Snake River an inland port,nearly 400 miles from the mouth of the Columbia River.

Whoa! Empty a link in the length of that chain of navigable water? Maybe? Just for a couple of weeks? Certainly not! Just a couple of days? Not likely.

The U.S. Army Corps of Engineers pretended to take the proposal seriously. Then rejected it. The brain trust was adamant that Celilo Falls would remain buried in its watery grave.

Still Klickitat County continued the battle.

The working title for the story was "Uncover Celilo Falls." The title of record is "Celilo Drain Plan."

The Story:

To see Celilo Falls as the site was before construction of The Dalles Dam, one must resort to skimpy footage and stills contained in historic archives. It is at this site on the Columbia where, archaeologists say, evidence points to it being a favorite fishing spot of Indians as early as 9,000 years ago.

Indians continued to fish on the huge runs of salmon at the famed cataract until the falls were inundated in 1957 by the rising reservoir behind the dam.

Today this stretch of the Columbia is a placid pool called Celilo Lake, the once-cascading falls buried by its 30-foot depth.

But if a group of Klickitat County residents has its way, the people would get to see the falls again. Why not drain the pool, they ask, and show the world Celilo Falls again, during Washington's centennial in 1989?

"We could turn back the technological clock," says George Rohrbacker, vice chairman of the centennial committee. "Maybe for just a couple of days." It would, according to Rohrbacker, give people a chance to experience "some of the things we've lost in our headlong rush into progress."

But the Corps of Engineers pulled the plug on the proposal, citing potential revenue losses, harm to fish, and structural damage to The Dalles and John Day dams.

However, Rohrbacker says the county committee will continue to lobby for the plan. He says its members will urge Washington and Oregon congressional delegations to help uncover the falls since it would be "an event of international magnitude."

An even more important aspect is how the Indians feel about it. They seem intrigued, but not a bit interested in sanctioning it. In fact, they indicate it would be a sacrilege. Something like digging into a grave.

One Indian spokesperson, Rita Dave, said "When the water covered the falls a lot of people's feelings were hurt. The old people cried."

At the time, Rita Dave was a youngster, eyewitness to the drowning of the falls. "I think about it a lot," she says. "And if they did that again, it would be like stabbing the people in the heart all over again."

Tim Wapato, Executive Director of the Inter-tribal Fish Commission, backed up that sentiment. "It could trigger some reminiscence of the resentment that was in Indian country at that time, and still exists, in the covering of those falls."

Still, proponents of the drawdown claim they do have some individual Indian support and will continue the battle...in the nation's capital.

Postscript:

127

The thought of seeing Celilo Falls again was grand. But that's it, a thought. The falls remain buried.

And remain renewed, only in memory.

Among the multitude of people who lament loss of Celilo Falls is The Dalles photographer/artist Wilma Roberts. Wilma has spent much of her life keeping the image of the falls alive. She has done this with use of old black-and-white photographs...her own and those of others...and painstakingly hand-tinted enlargements of the falls. It's her way of attempting to make tangible her memories of the site.

But as forceful and beautiful as she makes the photos, her own description of Celilo Falls is equally captivating.

"It was fantastic. It was just like a fairyland out there, because it was colorful, noisy, and misty."

Wilma's face flushes. She is giving away her secret. Her memories. "The falls made a noise like the ocean, the thunder of surf in a storm. And there was mist everywhere, and there would be rainbows in the mist."

She catches her breath, or is it a stifled sob? Her hand is poised above her head, then slowly drifts in an arc. "And you should have seen it all in early-morning light. Oh, it was splendid!"

Straight to the heart.

23   One-Man Co-op

Intro:

Laurie Campbell and Laurie McGuire, Albany, Oregon, high school chums...in fact, best friends...had a lot in common besides their first names. They often topped off conversations about their collective "alikes" with news that both their Dads were telephone company presidents. Jack McGuire, the one Laurie's father, headed up Albany's Bell Telephone Company. Allen Campbell, the other Laurie's dad, was boss of the McFarland Telephone Company in nearby Tangent, Oregon. But the playful punch line was always about a big dissimilarity that made Campbell's phone system unique. Especially in 1989.

The working title for the story was "Lone Phone." The title of record is "One-man Co-op."

The Story:

Allen Campbell of Tangent, Oregon, is the sole stockholder, customer, and officer of a 1920s rural telephone cooperative that once served about 15 farm homes. But as time passed, the McFarland Company dwindled, largely because the Bell System, to which the franchise had been sold, wouldn't allow the farmer line to add customers. By the same token, those already on couldn't be taken off.

Grandfathered in, they were.

"As people kept dropping off and dying off," says Campbell, "why, the lines got shorter and shorter, until finally, I was the only...if you'll pardon the expression...able-bodied member of the McFarland Telephone Company."

Allen served as both secretary and lineman when there were a couple of other co-op customers left. But now that they're gone, the extent of McFarland lines is from a utility pole in front of the Campbell home, running underground to the house, throughout the house, and to some of Allen's out-buildings. That's the sum of it.

And Allen chuckles, "I own the sole stock in the company." His eyes are amused, too. "I don't know where it is. But I own it. If I could ever find it." The glint is mischievous, infectious.

Still, Allen has to keep up the company records. The biggest part of that is filling out an annual form, filed with the Oregon Department of Revenue to maintain the company's tax-exempt status. How many miles of wire have been added each year?...Zero. How many new customers have been added?...Zero. Things like that go on the form.

But there is something new to report.

"Well, I thought after awhile, 'I think I deserve a promotion.'" Campbell teases, "So, I changed my title from secretary to president. So, I'm now president of McFarland Telephone Company."

And yes, Allen likes to be called "Pa Bell."

Postscript:

Allen Campbell did not make a living heading up a one-phone telephone company. Of course not. But he did do pretty well in the agricultural banking business. In retirement now, he and his wife, Nita, like to travel with their RV trailer to various encampments around the country.

However, Campbell remains active in the telephone company. His self-promotion to president still stands. There's no one to challenge that, of course. And he must still file those yearly reports, which takes a few minutes out of his retirement. New lines?...Zero. New customers?...Zero.

At this pace the McFarland Telephone Company and its president could last well into the 21st century.

24   The Painted Hills

Intro:

Millions of years ago volcanic action in central Oregon created a colorful landscape that people equate to the best of paintings. Or, at least, it seems they do. Why else would they call the area the "Painted Hills"? Or, to a cameraman like Ray Etheridge, they might be "magnificently picturesque."

Ray and I were on the road near John Day, Oregon, when we took a side trip through the hills. We had planned to only look, but we were moved to share a marvelous experience. In addition to our words and film, we set the experience to expansive music.

The working title for the story was "Master Painter's Hills." The title of record is "The Painted Hills."

The Story:

The Painted Hills of Oregon's John Day fossil beds are obviously the work of a master painter. The technique used here is the same as that seen in vistas the world over. But the Painted Hills are as different from a rain forest as the Sahara Desert is from a Congo jungle.

The hills gleam with reds, greens, ambers, grays, spots

of black. Whoever did this work used a huge brush, had a great eye for color.

However, some people believe it was a hurry-up job...perhaps took no longer than, say, a week. And, if so, that perhaps is why the Painted Hills have been constantly touched up for the past 20- to 30-million years.

Scientists say the canvas for the painted hills was spread out about that long ago. That there was a scatter of ash from volcanoes, ash transformed into clay by erosion. The clay, they say, will not hold water and offers scant nutrition; that's why plants do not grow here.

The experts also say they know why the Painted Hills change color as the weather changes. Rains turn the reds to pastel pink. And the amber to gold. Somehow, it seems, it would be the other way around. And, we're told, when the clay of the hills dries out, the surface cracks. The cracks then diffuse the light, turning what had been wet pink back to red; the gold back to amber. A master painter can work in mysterious ways.

Scientists, on the other hand, in their own way, have figured out the primary colors come from the presence of minerals, such as iron oxides that splash the dominant red around. Much the same as the minerals which give rust its color.

What does it matter? It is here. An eye-filling delight. A suffusion of striking hues, tinged by time and weather into a show that expands the emotions. It is, in a word...grand. Here in the Painted Hills of Oregon.
Postscript:

The Painted Hills are just one part of the John Day Fossil Beds National Park in Oregon. Sightseers tour it all, perhaps little wondering about which is more important: the fossils or the Painted Hills. The fossils tell of former life and geology. That's important, and most important to scientists. The Painted Hills unfold beauty. That's important, too, and most important to painters. Even to one <u>hanging in there</u>, making continual changes to what most people think is already a masterpiece.

25   McCall Was a Friend

Intro:

Both before and after Tom McCall served as Oregon's governor, he and I were coworkers at Portland broadcast stations. First at KGW radio in 1952 and again from 1975 through 1982 at the ABC affiliate television station KATU.

When you're living it, 30 years is a long time. And along the way if a colleague becomes governor, that's a source of pride. And friendships continue, of course, even though the friend has changed from reporting the news to making the news.

When Tom died of cancer in early January of 1983, Channel 2 News producers asked me to reminisce about McCall because we had known each other for such a long time.

We headed by car for the old McCall ranch near Prineville, Oregon, shortly before dawn. But we returned in the station's helicopter in order to make it in time for the early-evening news. For the first time ever I forgot to take along my portable typewriter. That was a blessing. Having to do longhand gave me a special feeling for the tribute.

Still, it was obvious to everyone who saw me close up on camera that it was one of the toughest assignments I had ever done. My voice betrayed that I was about to cry.

The working title for the piece was "McCall Eulogy."

The title of record is "McCall Was a Friend."

The Story:

Bright sunshine broke over the horizon of central Oregon today. A splash of happiness that tries to lighten the sorrow, a glow that tries to warm the cold heart of grief, a brilliance that challenges the solemnity of today and offers promise that it will not rain on Tom McCall's last parade.

So this is the ranch under the rimrock, the place where McCall grew up. So far from everywhere he learned to talk "funny"...for an Oregonian; the New England dialect of his parents, which stuck with him all his life. That rapid clip which some of us thought might, at any time, result in the biting off of some of those 75-cent words he often used.

So this is the place where Tom learned that immaculate articulation that made him so easy to understand. A foundation for a man who could describe a chest pain as a "lollapalooza." And his hope for Oregon that "she would not become a brazen, hungry hussy, giving herself to every stinking smokestack offered."

Only Tom McCall knows whether or not he will haunt this place. Somehow, it seems he already does.

And this is the place where Tom McCall will be buried at Redmond. Some others of his family are already interred here. His dad died in 1947, his mother just last year. They lie side-by- side. Nearby is the place where the governor will be laid to rest, next to brother Sam, who passed away in 1979.

The wind brushing this lonely place snaps the flag to

138

attention. And even at half-mast, it seems to whisper an apology for lack of a view.

These things are the only motion, the only sound, the only sight, that Tom McCall is to be buried here tomorrow.

I knew Tom McCall for 30 years. And you would think that after knowing someone that long you would know exactly what to say about him when he died. But to tell the truth, there is so much from which to choose.

There are some intimate details of McCall's life which have special meaning for me, because they relate to me. I could tell you about them, but I won't. They're my special treasure. However, I can tell you, that like all of you, I am sad about his death. I can't begin to describe my loss.

But at the same time, I'm happily snug in pride of having been a personal friend to the man who wrote some of the most important chapters in the book of Oregon history.

Postscript:

T. Lawson McCall and I shared a 15-minute spot for news at Portland radio station KGW back in 1952. I reported the news of the day, he did commentary. Only on the air was he T. Lawson, a combination of initial and name that not only had an authoritative ring to it, but was a bow to his mother as well. Dorothy McCall's maiden name was Lawson; her father, Thomas Lawson, was the famous, wealthy "Copper King" of Boston. Tom's paternal grandfather, Samuel McCall, once served in the U.S. Congress and also as governor of Massachusetts.

When he was not on the air, T. Lawson was known to everybody as simply, Tom. Tom McCall, who would one day be governor of Oregon.

I don't want to trace his political career. That's documented in history books, and his own autobiography. The short of it is that he was known as Oregon's "environmental governor" and one who welcomed visitors to the state conditionally, "for heaven's sake, don't stay."

After McCall's death, his desk in the newsroom stood unused, untouched. Weeks...perhaps a couple of months passed. The staff, reluctant to let go, treated the desk as if it were a shrine. Individuals would go there and stand before it, like visiting his grave, reading the epitaph. They did not sit in his chair, nor touch any papers.

But then, "Pat, we've got to do something about Tom's desk," said assistant news director Allan Anderson. "We want you to move there." Allan explained what I already sensed; it was an honor being bestowed on me. Still, I had to think about it a couple of days before I took occupancy. And over the next seven years before my retirement from Channel 2 in 1990, McCall's desk was my desk.

In deference to Tom, I tried to keep it as cluttered as he always did, even though I was never able to develop the instinct he had had for immediately locating any needed article in such disarray.

And sometimes while sitting there, looking like I was in deep concentration, I actually would be remembering. Maybe the time Tom sang at a benefit fund-raiser, torturing, I thought, "Ol' Man River" to death. Or when he was elected secretary of state and three of us, celebrants, pounded on his hotel room door at three a.m., expecting a drink. But got a deserved reprimand instead.

Or as governor when he stood like Moses, staff in hand, establishing the line separating Oregon's 300 miles of public-owned beaches from private land. Or his defusing of confrontation between American Legionnaires and anti-war protesters in Portland by sponsoring a rock festival encampment away from the city. Or his battle to keep military nerve-gas weapons from being stored in Oregon. Or his Bottle Bill. Or the frankness with which he kept the people informed about his battle with cancer. Or the first day he walked into the newsroom, a newsman again, after his two terms as the state's chief executive.

Or the night of his funeral services in the state capitol, where reporter Cathy Kiyomura hugged me and praised my McCall tribute and cried, and I did, too. But where the memorial was so upbeat and joyful that one could have imagined Tom was alive, not dead. Or the moving report next day by newsman Paul Hanson, when McCall was buried.

You get a lot to think about when you inherit a governor's desk.

26   Blind Broadcasters

Intro:

Winds blustered down the Columbia River Gorge in early autumn, as they always do, carrying to the careful listener the footfalls of the moccasins of winter. These gusts, though, gave no hint that, come spring, they would be joined by a throng of scantily clad transients, their Olympian bodies baked bronze by the sun, scooting along the river on boards with sails.

The September winds of 1984 were content to be joined only by the hum of a brand-new radio station: music, news, weather reports. All performed by people whose purpose was to make big waves. They were at work in Goldendale, Washington, on the Columbia.

Four members of the station staff had never ever actually seen the Columbia River, or a wind-surfing, bikini-clad body. Not because they wouldn't like to, but because they couldn't. They were blind. But they thought they could see a bright future as broadcasters.

The working title for the story was "Sightless Deejays." The title of record is "Blind Broadcasters."

The Story:

Kevin Malcolm notes the time, "KLCK news time 12:20..." echoing a voice he has just heard coming from a little black box. Kevin is the news director of one of the nation's newest radio stations, in Goldendale, Washington.

He's blind.

But then, so is the station's program director and morning disc jockey, Marty Lancer.

And so is Dennis Eisele, an intern at the station.

The chief engineer, Colin Malcolm, Kevin's brother, is also blind.

In fact, out of a staff of seven, KLCK has only three persons who can see.

The Malcolm bothers and Lancer, along with station manager Joe Henry, are the station's owners. Henry and sales manager Andy Ewing are both sighted and are part of a minority here which includes secretary Donna Chandler.

"We didn't intend to make this a haven for blind people," says Kevin Malcolm. "What has happened is that we have a group that knows how to make this a commercial market."

Andy Ewing was hired as sales manager because he has sight, "someone with more mobility." Andy creates a lot of the commercial copy and dictates it to the blind staffers, who type it in Braille. And both Andy and Donna Chandler write all copy in regular type for sighted staff members. And also provide copies for sponsors.

Even though Marty Lancer owns a piece of the action here, he says he'd like a "shot at the big time." And intern Dennis Eisele says he's getting experience to prove to other station bosses "that I'll be an asset, albeit a blind asset."

(segue to: 1987, Longview, Washington)

A blind disc jockey has taken over a prime-time slot, and his employer says he is doing such a good job he's headed for bigger things.

Dennis Hall (Eisele) is his name. Though he can't see he has something in common with radio; radio is also blind. That is, it lacks pictures, except in people's imagination. Still, it's difficult to imagine how a blind person could hold a job in radio, a medium of hundreds of buttons, switches, and knobs, thousands of labels, whirling tapes, and spinning discs. And uncounted lines of schedules and scripts. All of which, we would believe, takes eyesight to comprehend and work.

But here is 31-year-old Hall, popular country music deejay at Longview, Washington, radio station KBAM. Blind. But, probably, few of his fans know that.

Talent and determination, and a way of adapting radio to his blindness, have enabled Dennis to do the job.

"My first love is really sportscasting," says Dennis. "But I've developed a nice understanding and appreciation for country music. One of the things I like about it is that it's simple. You can tell at the beginning how it's going to end."

Like at Dennis' old station in Goldendale, commercials and interview questions are typed in Braille. Taped announcements receive Braille labels. But since joining KBAM eight months ago, Dennis's biggest project has been to catalog the station's entire record library in Braille. He's paid for some help out of his own pocket but also has had a lot of volunteer aid.

"The fact is," he says, "eyes that see are a big help to me; other people's eyes."

Other staff members help, too. One of the most important things is they read into a tape recorder the program log Dennis has to follow during his shift. Dennis keeps that handy on the console desk. And he tells time from a talking clock which he keeps in his pocket.

Dennis's bosses say he has "natural talent," is "polished," is an inspiration to others who see how much he has to do to get ready for the air.

Program manager Danny Houle says Dennis's job here at KBAM will be just a stepping stone in his career.

"He'll be frying bigger fish."

Postscript:

Marty Lancer, another of the Goldendale originals, struck out for the "big time," too. Lancer spent eight years at a Modesto, California, station, but then was caught in one of those changes of ownership squeezes. He bounced back with a new job in Stockton, where besides his duties as a host of "golden oldies" tunes, he was also named assistant program director.

Dennis Hall (now again Eisele) left Longview years ago, worked for a Merced, California, station, and now lives in Modesto. He and Lancer are in constant contact. Both say that new electronic technology has made it tough for them to keep a career in broadcasting. Digital radio has cramped their Braille style.

"Adaptive equipment is available," they say. "But it's awfully expensive."

Lancer further says, "Such equipment will talk, and tell where you are in a schedule on a computer screen. But even then, you're just asking for trouble if you expect a computer to work right every day, in every way." Lancer credits his wife of eight years, Terry, with being essential to his job.

"She is my eyes; works side-by-side with me; we split the salary. I'd be sunk without her."

Eisele still does recorded voice work for his old Longview station. However, a few years ago, he turned to telemarketing to earn a living.

The Malcolm brothers are still a team at Goldendale and now operate a second radio station there.

Since they first went on the air, over a dozen years ago, the Columbia River has become a vast playground in summer for wind-tossed acrobats on sailing surfboards. They can only imagine what that looks like, of course.

But when the winds of September whisper about fall, and later warn about the gales of winter, the hordes with all their flashy colors, the sails, the boards, the almost-clothes, disappear. They come here for the wind, and their own sense of wonder about the beauty of the Columbia Gorge. They think they have it all.

But when they leave, the Gorge appears again in its own incredible splendor, adorned and enriched by nature. It's not that the summer celebrants take the Columbia Gorge for granted. They don't. They appreciate its grandeur and as a place to play. But I'll bet not nearly as much as these blind broadcasters would if they could only see. Suddenly see.

150

27   PeeWee Rodeo Champ

Intro:

Kaelyn Sharp tugged on the reins of her pony, her "pointy" boots digging into the soft, dung-spattered dirt of the arena. She was afoot, not yet mounted, but ready to do her best in her rodeo specialty. Considering she was just four years old, and something of a novice to "rodeoing," she was learning fast about goat-tail tying.

But right now, in this last of the season's rodeos, she was towing her horse across the field to congratulate T.R. Wilson.

Wilson, it was clear, was on his way to capturing his second consecutive All-Around Cowboy title.

The working title for the story was "Rodeo Kids." The title of record is "PeeWee Rodeo Champ."

The Story:

"Let's do it." T.R. Wilson slaps the side of his crash helmet. Urgent now, he repeats, almost a shout, "Let's do it!"

The gate bursts open, horse and rider leap into the arena together—the horse, hell-bent on parting company with the rider, the rider hoping he can stick on for at least eight seconds.

"T.R. Wilson," blasts the voice of the rodeo announcer,

"aboard Silver Linin'. This horse ain't never been rode; there ain't a cowboy he ain't throwed."

T.R. is out to make him eat those words. It's an eternity, but eight seconds later T.R. is still aboard the gyrating animal. An air horn blares the signal that T.R. has triumphed. He is plucked from the bucking pony's back by pickup riders, and safely back on his feet, with not a scratch or bruise, T.R. doffs his helmet to acknowledge cheers from the grandstands. Then he clamps on his own broad-brimmed cowboy hat.

T.R. Wilson is in top form today. And why not? T.R., that is, Teddy Wilson...just eight years old...has Paul Newman's eyes, Cissy Spacek's freckles, and a gap-toothed grin all his own, the gap being the loss of a couple of "baby" teeth.

Teddy is the Northwest PeeWee Rodeo Association's 1986 "All-Around Cowboy." And he seems well on the way to backing up that celebrity by copping this year's championship, here at the 1987 season's final rodeo in Tygh Valley, Oregon.

Except for the size of its players and bucking and riding stock, PeeWee Rodeo has all the appearance of a big-time, professional show. And certainly, some competitors take some big-time lumps.

Some of these kids get hurt. A wild calf sometimes will dump you in the dirt and then stomp on you. A foot caught in a stirrup can mean trouble, too. Even a good ride can be embarrassing. Like the time John Miles rode a bucking horse to time, but in the next lurch was bounced into the air minus his boots. The boots and barefoot John all hit the ground at about the same time.

It's a sport of hard knocks; the kind of knocks that are far more than "kid stuff." But the kids keep coming back for more.

There's a wide range of age amongst contestants. And so, of course, there are various age groups in PeeWee competition. T.R. Wilson vies in a division that includes kids up to ten years old.

Teens are set apart in junior and senior divisions. So that means there'll be other champions crowned, too, after results of this contest are tabulated.

Some of these competitors are downright huggable. Take four-year-old Kaelyn Sharp, for example. Her specialty is goat-tail tying, a contest of time in which the object is to firmly tie a flashy ribbon to the thrashing tail of a goat. It isn't easy. And Kaelyn knows to get the job done, you most times have to hug the goat, too.

And then there's Teddy's younger brother, Jesse, who just this year started barrel racing. Jesse is not yet three years old. But he sits in a saddle much like his older brother, and also does the barrel race.

To become top all-around, Teddy competes in all events: bareback pony riding, calf riding, pole bending, goat tying...in addition to the barrels.

It all takes sacrifice. "Well, 'rodeoing' is tough work," T.R. says authoritatively. "And you have to practice a lot."

Shelves in the Wilson home at Philomath, Oregon, fairly well strain under the weight of prizes he's won. Belt buckles, statues, pictures, trophies, all attesting to his winning ways.

Of course, the capper is the second All-Around Cowboy saddle to go with the one he received last year. Back-to-back championships. So, how does T.R. feel about all this?

"Wel-l-l-l," he drawls, "I feel purty good."

Postscript:

Teddy Wilson was to become an even brighter star in PeeWee Rodeo. He won the All-Around Cowboy titles in both 1988 and 1989, making him a real phenomenon in the ranks of kid rodeo performers. Four championships in a row.

Like any top athlete, he gave a lot of the credit to his coach, Roger Wilson. Yes, that's right, his dad.

And as with all athletes, there came a time when the roar of the crowd was not enough. T.R."Teddy" Wilson quit rodeo some years ago, maybe when he was 12 or so. Now a young man, he thinks rather than be a rancher, he would like to be a logger.

Meanwhile, his dad continues to coach, or more accurately, train, animals. Roger Wilson is noted for uncanny ability to teach horses and mules all sorts of tricks.

One of his best students, a pinto horse, will play dead after supposedly being shot. The horse is sometimes a feature of the famed Pendleton Roundup's Happy Canyon show. During a battle between...what else?... cowboys and Indians, the "shot" pinto lies still until the end. Then, happily, gets up and limps off the field (really).

But Roger's most satisfying work is for the benefit of

154

people who are bound to wheelchairs. Paralytics who want to ride horses. Roger has trained, and is still training, horses and mules to lie down so such persons can actually mount from their wheelchairs. It is a way to get some legs back under them.

New legs. Four big, sturdy legs. Poor substitutes for their own, of course, but, nonetheless, legs that can take them over fields and ridges and through forests.

Where a wheelchair cannot follow.

28   Jugs of Help

Intro:

Sexton Mountain Pass was a killer. That's how Tom Evans of Sunny Valley, Oregon, saw it. Even though the pass tops out at a puny 1,960 feet, Tom knew how vehicles struggle to get over its summit.

Not because of snow or ice or wind or rain. No, those are given encounters, to be expected. What Evans discerned was that something could be done about the toll taken by summer heat. Stalled vehicles, gasping like lost prospectors, he reasoned, could be coaxed to life again with water.

In the late 1980s, jugs of water began to appear along that stretch of Interstate 5 freeway. Tom's doing, of course. Every kind of vehicle (cars, motor homes, pickups, trucks, and even some motorcycles) that stalled on the climb to Sexton Pass benefited because of Tom Evans.

Evans, Good Samaritan, was on the right track. But he stalled, too.

The working title for the story was "Thirsty Road." The title of record is "Jugs of Help."

The Story:

A heart attack has taken the Good Samaritan of Sexton Mountain out of action. But friends have taken over the responsibility of supplying jugs of water to treat the thirst of heat-exhausted vehicles on the steep I-5 climb.

Motorists traveling Interstate 5 on Sexton Mountain, a dozen miles north of the city of Grants Pass, Oregon, have a lot to worry about. It's here, that from both north and south, travelers encounter a steep, six-percent grade. In summer heat, that kind of slant seeks out weaknesses in all vehicles. It takes its toll: overheating engines, boiling radiators, stalling cars and trucks.

Scott Longstreet, from somewhere down the road, is a victim "We ran out of gas," he says. "And before we could switch to the reserve tank, the motor also got hot...really hot."

But not to worry. On this steep grade there's always a water jug handy. In fact, groups of jugs, about every quarter of a mile. They're put there by volunteers of the Sunny Valley Grange and Wolf Creek Alliance Church. Right now, Peggy and Joan Satow...mother and daughter...are making the deliveries.

Peggy and Joan are following another Good Samaritan who had to give up the work following a heart attack and open heart surgery. They make sure, as he did, that there are about 70 gallons of water distributed along six miles of the Sexton Climb.

"We usually go up on Fridays, just before the weekend,"

says Joan Satow. "You know, get plenty of water up there. Then we do it again on Mondays, for any travelers that may get overheated during the week."

Some people take the jugs. That's all right, according to the Satows. "If they have a really leaky radiator, they're going to need more water, and bottles to put more water in."

Motorists who, but for the well-placed jugs, would be stranded, do show their appreciation. The water pours out. Letters of thanks pour in.

"As long as there is the need," says Joan, "we'll be here to help, as long as we can."

More good news. The Satows may soon get help. The original jug man, Tom Evans, is on the mend. He thinks he might get his doctor's okay to return.

"I know it has to be done," he says. "Because there's too many people boil out goin' up that hill."

Postscript:

Tom Evans never did go back to jug delivery. His doctor advised against it. But sometimes, good deeds are catching. Perhaps the setting out of water jugs along a busy freeway can be compared to missionary work. It has a purpose, an aim, a goal...to help.

The effect of Tom's initiative along this stretch of I-5 is that other volunteers, principally the Sunny Valley Grange, have continued the work. The Grange to this day is still placing the jugs of help along Sexton Mountain Pass, rotating the duty amongst its members.

So from Memorial Day through Labor Day, the hot

summer season, relief is brought to overheated cars and steamed tempers by these good-willed water carriers. The jugs are stamped "do not drink," a precaution against vandals.

John Vial, a spokesman for the Oregon Department of Transportation, says that technically "no one is supposed to put things on the side of the road, the right of way. But we're not going to stop them. It's a Good Samaritan thing."

Beneficiaries of the jugs leave messages..."You saved my truck," said one. "Thank you, water elves," wrote another.

Not only that, but in this area where the Klamath Mountains and Siskiyou Range kind of crunch together, water jugs have begun to appear on other passes. There's Smith Hill and Stage Road Pass to the north, both of which get a share of jugs. And there's the Siskiyou Summit to the south, more than twice the height of any of the others at 4,310-feet elevation, but actually a longer, more gradual and easier climb.

One must understand, though, why Sexton is the toughest, and the spot where most breakdowns are likely to occur.

Running south on I-5 at Canyonville, the climb over the mountains to Grants Pass begins. Ten miles of uphill carries to the summit of Canyon Creek (elevation 2,020). That's enough to make a cranky car even crankier. Even about seven miles of flat after the Canyon Creek summit might not be enough to give a faltering vehicle a breather in time for the next obstacle, the climb to Stage Road Pass (elevation 1,830). But then there's another, less than four miles away...Smith Hill Summit (elevation 1,730). And a lot of ups and downs between.

Suddenly, there's Sunny Valley, but it's just a short dip before the abrupt ascent to Sexton Pass (elevation 1,960). It is on the short downhill run to Sunny Valley that experienced truckers let their rigs roll, picking up speed to attack the last big rise between them and the city of Grants Pass.

Motorists do the same. They are gritting their teeth, hoping their vehicles will be able to make the final sharp climb on Sexton Mountain. Most do. Many do not. It depends on the health of the vehicles.

The jugs are waiting.

29   Fremont Bridge Flags

Intro:

It's a brave and dedicated crew that keeps "Old Glory" flying high on top of the Fremont Willamette River Bridge in Portland, Oregon.

The American and Oregon flags that fly 400 feet up on the rainbow arch of the Fremont were meant to be only a U.S. Bicentennial event, back in 1976.

But public demand forced their permanent display, which also put in motion the need to constantly change the flags.

The working title for the story was "Fremont's Old Glory Yet Waves." The title of record is "Fremont Bridge Flags."

The Story:

It makes one proud to see the U.S. and Oregon flags waving over the city, so high up. From anywhere in town that you can see the Fremont Bridge, you also can see the banners of country and state.

Trouble is, the Northwest winds that whip along the Willamette River tear at the flags something fierce. So every few weeks the Oregon highway maintenance department sends up a couple of workers to take down the tattered flags and replace them with new ones.

"We try to pick a day that's not too windy," says crewman Ed Miller. "From down here the flags look deceptively small, but they're so big that if a strong gust of wind hit it, Old Glory could knock you right off the top of the bridge."

Obviously, changing of the flags is not one of Miller's favorite assignments. But his sidekick today, Richy Maes, thinks it's great. "The wind aside," he says, "I really enjoy it. From up there you can see all over the city."

The wind-battered flags are repaired right in Portland at the shop of McGee Awning and Blind Company. The frayed ends are cut off and patches sewn to tears. (Patches are things you don't see from the road level, of course.)

The Star Spangled Banner is easier to fix than our own state flag. Shop owner George Trotter says that's because the Oregon flag is double-paneled, has two emblems, and a lot of lettering to replace.

The flags start out about 20-by-30 feet. When the constant fraying reduces the length to anything under 28 feet, they're discarded. Still, their maintenance costs only about $125 a year.

It is not always Miller and Maes who change the Fremont flags. But whoever does it has to have guts and stamina to get up there. These guys have to climb inside the steeply arching main girder, as if exploring a narrow cave. But instead of crawling over rocks, they must wriggle through numerous bulkhead joints to reach the top.

It's a strenuous ascent of over 200 feet. And when they

get there, they're twice that distance from the surface of the river. Ed and Richy offered to take us along. But fortunately, our helicopter was already in the air to photograph them at the top, so they had to hurry along without us. A spelunker I am not. Whew!

So, unfurled here is the latest change of the Fremont flags. The red, white, and blue of Stars and Stripes; the blue and gold of the Beaver State...flexing in the rising wind. And Miller and Maes make ready to climb down again.

Both men say there's a bonus for this dangerous duty. Money? No, of course not. "Pride!"...in keeping Old Glory flying over this part of the "land of the free and the home of the brave."

Postscript:

It all occurred during the Ides of March. No...not the assassination of Julius Caesar...at least not in this case. It was the birth of the Fremont Bridge across the Willamette River in Portland, Oregon. More accurately, it was the raising of the center span of the new bridge, a feat which took three days and was compared to the exactness of an Apollo moon shot.

KATU-TV Manager Tom Dargan set in motion Channel 2's live coverage of the event. We were actually convened in a Monday morning editorial board meeting, but Dargan shifted attention to the Fremont. He wanted live coverage, and he knew just how to get it. Our station didn't have a live remote truck, but sister station KOMO in Seattle did. And that truck was right then returning to Seattle from covering a sports event in Eugene.

"God, Tom," editorial writer Bruce Baer said. "Watching that center span go up will be something like watching grass grow."

"Or paint peel," volunteered anchorman Rick Meyers.

"Boring," chimed in public affairs director Ted Fore.

I looked at Dargan to see if I could tell whether he was joking, or what. I couldn't tell, but as it turned out he was downright serious. We were there to vote on proposed editorial stands, but it was obvious we were not going to get to vote on the Fremont coverage. "It'll be fun," he said. "Let's do it. Intercept that truck."

So in March 1973, we "tore people away from watching their trees and grass grow and paint peel" to be eyewitness to completion of the new bridge.

It was slow, but Dargan was right. It was also fun. The center of the bridge, all 16,000 tons of it, was constructed a mile downstream, and then brought into place by tugboats. Positioned across the river it was then hoisted by giant jacks, clusters of threaded rods that slowly inched the huge piece upward into place. Night and day for nearly three days we did almost hourly reports, with Meyers anchoring from the deck of a floating restaurant.

A part of the coverage that scored highest for interest (and still does today) was a time-lapse film made by Murl Shick of Longview, Washington.

Shick, who simply volunteered, started shooting a frame a minute shortly after the center span was floated upriver. And as it was swung into place and raised, he continued

166

photographing to come up with unique footage. It covers in about a minute and a half what it took engineers over two and a half days to do. That footage is still in Channel 2 and Oregon Historical Society archives.

Three years later, during the nation's bicentennial, flags of both America and Oregon were unfurled atop the highest arch of the Fremont. They are still there because a dedicated crew keeps them flying.

30   Quigley's Fame

Intro:

The National Cowboy Hall of Fame at Oklahoma City added Portland western artist Edward Quigley to its roster early in 1984. The honor surprised Quigley, but not his friends.

Quigley was "on his last legs," seriously ill but still mobile and working when the recognition came.

Photog Don Stapleton and I were greatly impressed by the artist's determination to continue painting, despite poor health, and his regrets about having had to give up smoking to have any health at all.

He was, we discerned, as gruff as we had heard, but also as sensitive as you would expect an artist has to be.

The working title for the story was "Quigley's Call to the Hall of Fame." The title of record is "Quigley's Fame."

The Story:

Edward Burns Quigley..."Quig"...nowadays has a replica of the Charles Russell bronze sculpture "Night Rider": the trophy that goes along with being inducted as a wrangler into the Cowboy Hall of Fame.

"I never got into competition in art," muses Quig, "I just

wasn't all that much interested."

But obviously Quigley, along the way, won a national reputation. The worth of his work is not only highlighted by the hall of fame, but the fact that since 1975 a complete gallery of the Oregon Historical Society has exhibited his art.

Quig is best known as a painter. But as a wood carver he also ranks among the best. The exhibit displays representative work of both, from about the time he was in the second grade through to the present.

Society Director Tom Vaughn, who represented Quig at the induction ceremony, put it this way: "Naturally, Oregonians are awfully pleased about Quig's honor, and it is recognition that he so richly deserves."

Quigley says he never considered himself to be a cowboy, a buckaroo. "I simply went along on cattle drives and roundups of wild horses, and painted."

His favorite painting is one he did of Indians rounding up wild horses during the depression years on the Yakima, Washington, reservation.

His home mirrors his talent, completed works sharing space with those just started.

Quig, now 88 years old and ailing, most of the time trails an oxygen tube that helps ease his emphysema. And that's why he couldn't go to Oklahoma City. It's also why he now gets up strength to work only a little at a time. But recently he completed a painting on one of his favorite themes...the old-time circus.

It's early morning, long before dawn. Oil-fueled wicks

light the road to the grounds. And two young boys have joined the parade of horse-drawn wagons. They are excited, happy. They might get free admission if they help relay the lamps to the head of the troop.

One of the boys is Quig. The same Quig who is now a wrangler in the National Cowboy Hall of Fame.

Postscript:

We were through, so we broke down the gear, folded the camera and lights tripods, and packed away the camera and tapes. Quigley reinserted the oxygen nose piece he had removed for our interview, so he could again breath better.

His wife produced cups of coffee and some cookies and urged us to stay awhile longer. We could not refuse.

I walked around the room, looking again at Quig's work. I paused in front of the circus scene. I thought of a question I should have asked when we had Quig on camera, "Which one of the kids is you?"

Quig slowly got up from his chair, and just as slowly walked across the room, the oxygen tube snaking along behind him. Finally, he stood beside me, staring at the painting. His hand touched my shoulder. He grinned.

"Either one."

31   Hall Family Cave

Intro:

"Shorty" Hall would not come with us to the place he called "the cave place." Nor would he allow us to call him by his given name, Otho. His father's name was Otho. It seemed Shorty did not like his father much, so he didn't like the name either.

In 1984 Shorty Hall was 74 years old and on the tail-end of a lifetime of cattle roundups and breaking horses. A cowboy, a buckaroo. And finally, a sort of horseback security guard for a logging outfit in a forest near Rice Hill, Oregon.

But Hall was also a surviving member of a huge family that spent many years living in an eastern Oregon cave, somewhere in the vicinity of the tiny town of Drewsey.

Hall's photo album disclosed a lot about his life in the cave. "Bad memories," he said. "I never go there."

The place is now called the Hall family cave, and is so remote a 4-wheel-drive vehicle is sorely tested to get to it. And a local guide carries a gun to defend against rattlesnakes.

"If we see any (snakes)," he says, "I want you to know they're damn hard to hit...when you're shooting over your shoulder."

It was the only humor in covering the story whose

working title was "Cowboy Album." The title of record is "Hall Family Cave."

The Story:

This huge cave near Drewsey, Oregon, harbors some tragic memories of a pioneer family: a cave that was a home for more than three decades around the turn from the 19th to the 20th century.

The summer sun grips this forsaken place, warning not even a breeze to stir. Even the ghosts here are intimidated. The tumble-down relics bake in the heat, and refuse to tell about the family who lived here. Or so it seems at first glance.

But then the mind's eye penetrates the blotchy shimmer to learn that the remains of this curious dwelling, though apparently mute, are whispering. Faint murmurs say "Yes, they were here." Or maybe, "...we are here."

The 12-by-24 foot cave might have been grand for ancient man, but one can only wonder why Otho Hall chose it for a home in 1885. Especially for a wife and 11 kids.

It was here the creek robbed the Halls of a two-year-old daughter...drowned in a stream that today barely has a trickle of life itself.

Hall and his wife, Rebecca, separated. The children scattered. But that wasn't the end.

Otho Hall remarried, brought his bride, Charlotte Maxfield, to the cave, and began a new family.

The determination with which the Hall family tried to

make this forlorn outcrop of rock into a home is pointed up by their building of a rock wall. It served to not only pretty up the place, but also as a foundation for construction of a wood frame extension of their home. A kitchen.

Pictures of 1916 show the children of the second family: Otho, named for his father, and daughters Daisy and Lucy, framed against the lean-to kitchen at the cave's entrance.

It was about this time tragedy struck again. A pistol Mrs. Hall carried for protection while working in her garden slipped out of the holster, dropped to the ground and discharged. The bullet struck her, but she clung to life for 21 days before she died.

Hall married a third time. But that didn't last. And for a brief period of time the three kids were wards of the Boys and Girls Aid Society. The Society was primitive. That's an Oregon convict boot on little Lucy.

That was the end of it. The Halls abandoned the cave in 1923. In the 60 or so years since then, sagebrush and other hardy shrubs have claimed the yard. Time and weather have combined to collapse the skimpy wooden kitchen facade. And the cave is empty.

But can it be, really...empty?

Postscript:

Cameraman Don Stapleton, field technician George Avila, and I were uncomfortable at the "cave place." Not for fear of rattlesnakes. Not because of the heat. There was some other reason to look over our shoulders. But what? As we left there was the urge to quicken the pace, but concomitant with that feeling was the desire to turn back, to linger. We shot backward looks long after the Hall family cave was out of sight.

But I could not help but think, like Shorty Hall, that it would be a good thing not to go there again.

178

32   Mustangs Range

Intro:

The first mustangs to run free in the wide open spaces of western America were the horses of the Spanish conquistadors. But over the intervening centuries, lost, strayed, or stolen horses from many other sources contributed to the scores of wild horse herds that roam western rangeland today.

Mustangs want to be left alone. And there are people who say they should be left alone. But this wild bunch, these mustangs, although tracing their roots back to the 1500s, has overreached through over population.

They are pests, some say, competing with domestic livestock for forage on the open range.

Wild-horse control fell into the responsibility of the Bureau of Land Management. And that Fed agency has struggled since the 1970s to keep the range open for cattle grazing by removing mustangs from their home on the range. But leaving some mustangs at home, to range free.

The working title for the story was "Wild Horse Roundup." The title of record is "Mustangs Range."

The Story:

A helicopter noisily bounces along just above the juniper, so close to the ground it soon is clattering just above the eastern Oregon sagebrush. It twists, darts to there, back to here, to-and-fro. The huge rotor blades whip up swirls of dust that mingle with clouds of dust kicked up by frightened horses, running for their lives.

Wild horses. Mustangs. Broomtails. Whatever they're called, they're a problem. Basically because they compete with domestic livestock for forage on the open range. Consequently, since the mid-1970s, roundups like this have been going on to reduce wild- horse herd populations. The mustangs are driven to trapping corrals by helicopter and then the trap is closed by mounted buckaroos to make sure they stay there.

Prior to passage of the Wild Horse and Burro Protection Act of 1971 the surplus horses went two ways: the good ones were kept for work, the "culls" were sold to slaughterhouses.

Now they go only one way: through the Bureau of Land Management's Adopt-A-Horse program. But over the past several years there has been a growing number of these horses nobody wants: the old, the lame, the sick, the ugly. And the so-called "knotheads" that are not trainable. These horses have become an ever-increasing problem for the BLM.

BLM district manager Josh Warburton says about 30 percent of wild horses are not adoptable, and four BLM facilities in the West are currently simply holding and feeding these unwanteds.

"I think we may reach a point," says Warburton, "where we've just got too many unadoptable horses."

The BLM has no problem finding homes for most horses, including true mustangs, horses believed to be "Spanish Barbs" descended from horses brought to the new world by the conquistadors. The kind of horse that comprised the great herds of the plains Indians, and was the tough little cow pony of the old west. But they are only a small portion of the wild herds of today. But what is to become of what the BLM calls the "unadoptables?"

Well, Josh Warburton says he thinks horse lovers are coming around to an idea most abhorred a few years ago: that they would become horse meat. Horse meat, according to Warburton, is staple fare on tables of some European and Asian countries. And it is likely, too, some horses would be rendered for dog food.

Warburton himself cringes at the thought. "But obviously the situation we're in can't go on forever and ever."

A bill that would allow the BLM to sell the old, the lame, the sick, the ugly, and the knotheads for such purposes has stalled in this 1986 session of Congress. Meanwhile, trimming of the wild-horse herds continues, while the stockpile of unwanted mustangs continues to grow.

Postscript:

Oregon's wild-horse problems got a lot better in just a few years. The BLM's horse adoption program ultimately caught the public fancy, and by 1989 the state had a waiting list of people who wanted mustangs.

The BLM wranglers not only were able to reduce mustang populations, but began to manage herds for quality and character: at Palomino Butte, a herd of palominos; an appaloosa herd in a different part of the range; the Spanish Barbs, of course, whose range is in the Kiger Gorge of Oregon's lofty, mystical Steens Mountain.

In July of 1989 the chief of the BLM's division of wild horses, John Boyle, cited Oregon's wild-horse operation as "exemplary," at the dedication of the Kiger range viewpoint.

As it turned out there was no need to cull herds by slaughter for overseas diners or dog dishes. But it was a game of catch-up until a point was reached where the state's herds could be held at desired levels by roundups of only several hundred animals a year.

For a time the real outcasts, the unwanted, were sent to a sort of "retirement home," a range in Montana. And the older horses were simply neutered and returned to the local range.

Dean Bolestad, currently the man in charge of the wild-horse program in the Burns BLM district, says Oregon, fortunately, had fewer wild horses to contend with than some other states, such as Nevada. In other western states with larger herds, horses are still being shipped to holding facilities. The most notable of these is at Bartlesville, Oklahoma. And, as of this writing, Oregon has gotten a bit behind and is faced with the prospect of again having to reduce its wild-horse population to what Bolestad calls "appropriate managing numbers." Bolestad says Oregon range mustangs now total about 3,000 head, and future roundups have a goal of reducing that number to around 2,100 horses. Manageable.

Now in Oregon there are about 20 wild-horse herds, most of which are not of pure Spanish descent. But all of which romantically fit the name mustang.

33   Frog Champs

Intro:

The frog's name was Dan'l Webster and he was a champ, could "outjump any frog in Calaveras County," it was claimed. But a "double handful" of quail shot, surreptitiously poured down Dan'l's gullet by a nefarious stranger, sort of anchored him, as Mark Twain put it, "planted solid as a church." And the "notorious jumping frog of Calaveras County" lost.

Twain's story also was a lesson: Never leave your jumping frog with a stranger who says if he had a frog he would agree to bet you $40 his frog would outjump your frog, and you go off somewhere to catch a frog for him to prove him wrong. If you expose your overconfidence and greed and trust like that, a stranger can take advantage of your frog while you're away, and you, when you return with his frog.

The appeal of the tale is evergreen, and, to this day, gets an annual surge of new life when Angels Camp, California, celebrates its notoriety during the month of May. The focus, of course, is on round after round of frog-jumping contests.

Oregon entrants won the big event many times over the years. So, in 1987, when an Oregon competitor named Sugar Town Dandy beat out all other frogs for the Calaveras

County title, I imagined it was important.

The working title for the story was "Oregon Frog Cops Calaveras Crown." The title of record is "Frog Champs."

The Story:

John Hand of Sweet Home, Oregon, is a "frog jockey" and captain of the Oregon frog jumping-team that has tended to dominate the Calaveras County frog-jumping competition at Angels Camp, California. And here he is, at one of the ponds near his Sweet Home home, demonstrating one of the techniques for capturing potential champion jumping frogs.

It seems to be almost as much fun as the jumping competition itself. Dangle a bright cloth bait on a blunted hook, and a bullfrog sees red. He jumps, snaps, and gets hoisted, captured, all in split seconds.

But just how do you tell a champion-calibre frog from an ordinary frog?

Easy, according to Hand, they have to have good legs. "You know, you see a girl once in awhile whose legs seem to run clear up to her shoulders? Well, that's what I look for in a frog. That frog is going to Calaveras County."

John's entry, Sugar Town Dandy, won the jumping competition at Angels Camp with a total distance in three successive jumps of 19 feet, 7 and one-quarter inches. John says the winner was caught, along with other Oregon entries, on location near Angels Camp and was released back into his remote mountain pond soon after the contest.

The rules allow for any entry to be from anywhere, so

186

that's why a California frog is the Oregon champ.

A frog entered by John's daughter, Debbie, won at Angels Camp in 1982. Another of the Oregon team, Janet Seiber, won in 1984 when her frog, Weird Harold, set a world record leap of 21 feet, one and one-half inches. That record stood for two years.

John's win is number three in the last six years. But it hasn't all been win, win. High hopes for the championship one year were literally crushed when a team member accidentally stepped on the frog sack. Another year the frogs were prostrate from the heat, after they unknowingly worked their sack from the shade into hot sunlight.

But one of the biggest jobs in frog competition, says daughter Debbie, is the naming of the contestants.

"We're talking about 100, maybe 200 frogs, all needing names at once," Debbie says. "And they gotta have names that fit their personality. It's tough, so we all gather around and make suggestions. But, sure, it's still fun."

It's also noteworthy that Oregon has captured the Calaveras contest's governor's trophy for many years. The trophy won by a frog jumping for Governor Neil Goldschmidt will soon be presented to our chief executive by the Oregon team.

What was that frog's name? "Comeback Croaker."

Soon the Oregon champs will be recruiting frogs for the jumping contest held in conjunction with the town of Jefferson, Oregon's mint festival. But the frogs should be advised that someone in Jefferson has come up with some mint recipes which include frog legs.

Postscript:

187

It seems the Oregon frog team peaked in 1987. As of this writing, they've not won a championship at Angels Camp since then. And they didn't even go to Calaveras County a couple of years.

"Several times we've had frogs that had the longest jumps in the preliminaries," declares John Hand. "But then they'd poop out in the finals."

But Hand blames himself. "Mismanagement," he says. "Things like, if a frog was too cold, we couldn't get it warmed up. If it was too warm, we couldn't get it cooled down."

A real heartbreaker, though, came in 1996. A big Oregon female frog shattered the world record, jumping 21 feet, 11 1/2 inches in the preliminaries. There was much joy in the Oregon camp at Angels Camp. The smell of a new championship. But then, there came another mishap.

When Hand lifted the lid of the frog container "she shot out of there like a canon," like she was already in the arena.

"It could be, too," Hand says, "she simply wanted to get away. All frogs want to get away. That's why they jump. That's why they have such long legs."

Hand maybe overreacted; to thwart what he believed was an escape attempt, rather than zeal, on the part of his frog to get on with the contest, he grasped her firmly...with both hands.

"I squeezed her some," says Hand, with a hint of

remorse and apology in his voice, "and she went into a funk. I don't know if I hurt her, or just injured her pride. Anyway, in the finals her spirit was gone, she jumped only 16 feet."

And things have gotten worse: John can't even remember her name.

34 Harney Basin Flood

Intro:

In the early 1980s strange weather descended on Harney county, Oregon, an area of high sagebrush desert. Unusually deep snowpack and heavy spring runoff began to expand Malheur Lake into marshes of its huge game refuge and ranchers' hayfields.

As the cycle continued for four or five years, Malheur Lake spilled through a trough called "The Narrows" into Harney Lake, and inundated long sections of major roads and the Burns/Hines rail line.

Slowly, over the years, the water rose some eight feet above what would be normal high water. Fish were swimming in the sagebrush, trying to spawn on a highway. At least 30 ranches had to be abandoned, their ruins scattered around the lakes.

It was not a flood like a torrent of water rushing through an area, but an agonizingly torpid consumption of terrain and buildings. The sluggishness of the flood, however, did not make it any less a disaster.

Yet, in the winter of 1985, four years after the start of the problem, the Harney Basin was still not considered a disaster area by the federal government.

At that time we did one of what was a continuing series

of reports on the situation. The working title for the story was "Burns Flood Folo." The title of record is "Harney Basin Flood.

The Story:

Winter ice has contained the rise of floodwaters across the Harney Basin until spring. But the relentless flow over the past four years has expanded Malheur, Harney, and Mud Lakes to some 180,000 acres. Thirty ranches have been inundated in the normally shallow, 70,000-acre marsh.

Local industry has lost railroad service; highways have been damaged. County Judge Dale White says damage last year reached $32.7 million.

"With the spring melt," says Judge White, "the water will just keep coming. We expect it will ruin many more acres of land."

The only bright spot in all this misfortune was when people here banded together to save a historic one-room schoolhouse. It was moved from a spot now underwater, up along this road, to high ground. But, of course, a lot more was involved than simply saving the building.

A half-dozen youngsters attend the Sod House school. They had to abandon the building last year when the rising water lapped at the steps.

But then, a community effort of sales, fund drives, and donations collected enough money to salvage the structure and move it to a location high on this hill overlooking Malheur Lake.

The only other alternative would have meant the kids

would have had to travel 60 miles a day to attend school in Burns.

The flood is relentless, even in winter. Ice buildup around utility poles has put on pressure that has snapped main transmission lines. Harney County Electric Cooperative is constantly at work, repairing damage.

Back in 1982, Governor Vic Atiyeh declared the county a disaster area. But the Feds have refused to go along.

Right now, though, the U.S. Army Corps of Engineers is studying a possible solution: the building of a canal through the Malheur Gap to the south fork of the Malheur River, to drain the basin. The study should be completed by spring. But even if approved, the project would not start until late 1987.

People here do not find much comfort in that.

Postscript:

Another consequence of the climatic change was that the vast Alvord Desert, in deep southern Harney County, once a prehistoric lake, became a lake again.

The Alvord Desert is a region of bubbling hot springs and long, long miles of flats, the place where, in 1976, Kitty O'Neil rocketed to a new land speed record for women drivers. And maybe could have broken the record held by a man, but was not allowed to try.

The Alvord Desert turned to 60,000 acres of shallow lake by 1984. Even the famed Alvord Ranch, at the foot of Steens Mountain and hugging the edge of the desert, lost several thousand acres of grassland to the new water.

It allowed one to see for the first time what prehistoric people saw: a lake, framed by immense expanse of earth and sky in a region whose beauty defies description. For awhile there, one could almost feel that past and present...now and then...were one.

But, despite all attempts to forecast what weather will do, weather, if nothing else, is unpredictable. In a complete about-face, nature recycled and in the late 1980s was drying out Harney County again...as slowly as it had sent in the water.

However, in 1988, a new problem glared. As the water receded, erosion of the flood and ice exposed a wealth of ancient Indian culture at both Malheur and Harney Lakes, near Burns. And relic hunters were making off with many of the artifacts, causing worry that a priceless archaeological legacy was being threatened.

George Constantino, then manager of the huge game refuge, called the relics "10,000 years' worth of ancient Indian population." He added that pot hunters had already raided many of the rich, new sites, along lakeshores and on islands exposed by the retreating water.

The Malheur raiders, according to Constantino, walked off with an amazing amount of cultural material, but apparently left exposed human skeletal remains where they lay.

The artifacts were like those commonly found throughout the high desert great basin, where primitive people lived in the shallow marshes for thousands of years. The relics' removal makes it virtually impossible for professional investigators to accurately trace the people's history.

Constantino wished that he could forge an "alliance with these people who are hobbyists, really serious amateurs, and get them working with us, to use their skills and knowledge." But what worked better to discourage the pot hunters were arrests and some convictions.

The small band of Paiutes of the tiny tribal reservation at Burns insisted that exposed human remains be reburied right where they lay. And that is what happened.

The study to drain floodwaters of northern Harney County through Malheur Gap was moot.

And far south, the desert sun, streaming down on the Alvord, created another dramatic transformation. The desert-turned-lake was turned back again to desert; thousands of acres of alkalai flats and swirling sands of the Alvord came into their own again, a place that could again be called desert, the Alvord Desert, a desert framed by immense expanse of earth and sky in a region whose beauty defies description.

And the Paiutes announced they would build a gambling Casino at Burns.

35 Statehouse Statue Gild

Intro:

High atop the Oregon Capitol, a gold-gilded figure glitters in the sunlight. A statue of a man, a pioneer. Not just any pioneer, mind you, but the embodiment of all Oregon pioneers. One can see the statue expresses the earliest days in Oregon history, from the arduous trek along the Oregon Trail to settlement of the new territory. It is also a symbol of adventure and determination, and strength of spirit, valuable in any time, including the present.

In 1983 that kind of spirit flowed from a tiny eight-year-old girl who came up with an answer to a problem the State Legislature could not solve. The weather-beaten Oregon pioneer statue needed a new coat of gold leaf. But the legislature just couldn't see where the money would come from to do the job.

Then third-grader Jenny Borden stepped in. She knew what to do. Kids all over the state, she believed, would be willing to help the "gold man." She was right. Lots of adults got the "pioneer spirit," too. And by the time Oregon's 125th birthday rolled around on February 14, 1984, things looked bright for the Pioneer.

The working title for the story was "Shabby Pioneer Rescued." The title of record is "Statehouse Statue Gild."

The Story:

197

The Oregon Capitol is alive today with the sound of hundreds of children's voices. Laughter, chatter. The sound of the future, ringing in austere chambers of government. Because of their youth, most probably see this building as awfully old. And certainly the object of need they've come to see is ancient...nearly 50.

The kids are here as representatives of tens of thousands of the state's school children who came through in a pinch. And thereby, they've helped solve one of Oregon's biggest problems in this 125th year of statehood.

You see, the Oregon Pioneer statue, that gold-gilded beacon that looks at us from the highest point of the Statehouse, a constant reminder of our heritage, this symbol of pride and confidence in our past, present, and future...is on hard times.

Well, actually, was on hard times. The gild on the Pioneer, you see, has been beaten by the elements. And, if you look close-up, as many visitors to the Capitol dome do, you see he is shabby. If left untended, the state of disrepair will be obvious even to people out on the mall.

The last couple of legislatures looked at the problem, but didn't tackle it. That would have meant coming up with $35,000 to $45,000 for the coating job. The attitude seemed to be that the Pioneer may be on hard times, but so is the state.

Well, that terrible admission was picked up on by a little girl right here in Salem. The rest is history.

The plaintive appeal of eight-year-old Jenny Borden

burgeoned into a statewide fund drive; the kids of the state came through. And doggone it, the Governor (Victor Atiyeh) has been handed a check as big as a poster, and which shows there's enough money to do the job.

Now, the Pioneer is not as old as some might think. The statue was one of the finishing touches to a building that replaced the Capitol that burned in 1935. There's even a record in pictures of the 8 1/2-ton, 24-foot-tall statue being hoisted to its perch on the dome.

We also have the good fortune to know all about its sculptor, Ulric Ellerhusen, and, more importantly now, who did the original gilding.

In 1938 and again in 1958, the gold was applied by A.M."Bob" Fulton of Portland. His son, Bob "junior" tells us his dad...now over 80 and a victim of Alzheimer's disease...kept a handwritten diary detailing all the materials and every step in the process.

The worth of the elder Fulton's work is pointed up by the fact that the first coat stood up a decade longer than estimated. After the second gild was done in 1958, it was expected a third would be added in 1978. So, we're a bit late.

Bob Fulton, Jr. says he will try to get the job.

Some among us may wonder why not just sandblast the statue down to the bronze and let it go at that. Hey, anyone who would suggest that ought to be ashamed. Especially in the view that Oregon's 125th birthday coincides with this year's Olympic Games.

Gold marks a winner; bronze, an also-ran. The plaster

of gold leaf made possible by the generosity of Oregon's kids is so much more than appearance, so much more than a symbol of riches. It is a bright-yellow, gleaming sign that says..."Oregon is a winner!"

Postscript:

The scaffold wrapped around the Pioneer Statue sways slightly as we climb up to see the gold gild work in progress. The motion is discomfiting. It helps some, though, that the scaffolding itself is sheathed in a cocoon of opaque plastic, making it impossible to see that you are 160 feet or so above the ground. Still, the wobble and a slight wind that slaps at the plastic cover keep you alert as to where you are, making it difficult to relax.

Mid-October 1984: the job of re-gilding the statue has been under way for nearly a month and is now nearly complete. Even on this dull day you can see there's nothing like a new suit of gold leaf to rekindle the spirit...of Oregon's Pioneer.

Artisans Roy Darby and John Edwards apply the feather-light gold leaf in small squares, just inches at a time, on a layer of special adhesive. Incredibly, the 24-foot-tall statue will be entirely covered with just 7 ounces of gold. But its 12,000 sheets, each just 1/200,000 of an inch thick, will protect the bronze core of the statue into the 21st century.

There's nostalgia here, too. Bob Fulton, Jr.'s Security Signs Company and Williamsen & Bleid, Inc...both Portland firms and both associated with gilding of the statue decades ago...are back again, doing the delicate work.

Wisps of gold, fluffed by the rubbing action that both secures and polishes the stuff, scatter now and then, settling like dust at the statue's feet.

A few days later, the bright new Pioneer is unveiled and gleams in the Oregon sun. And Oregon history is enriched by how it came about.

And as the 21st century loomed it seemed certain that that 1984 gold leaf would last into the new millennium. It did. And then, in the fall of the first year of the brand-new century and second millennium, when the time came for another new makeover for the Pioneer, there was none of the hassle that prompted little Jenny Borden's action. There was money left over from the $48,000 raised by the school kids' fund drive. There was profit from a state-operated gift shop. There was a bar of gold donated by a mining firm. Talented young artists from a new firm affixed the fresh coat of gold leaf in the old way. The Pioneer Statue continued to radiate, bouncing golden sun rays down the Capitol Mall.

Jenny Borden, the third-grade girl who prompted the Pioneer fund campaign, has always really been Jennifer Elizabeth Borden. But she's now called Miss Borden at Gaffney Lane Elementary School in Oregon City, Oregon. Yes, Jennifer is now a teacher. Miss Borden teaches second grade. And...oh, yes...also third grade.